An Essay on Pope

An Essay on Pope

FREDERICK M. KEENER

Columbia University Press

New York and London 1974

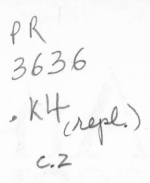

*The Andrew W. Mellon Foundation, through a special grant,
has assisted the Press in publishing this volume.*

Library of Congress Cataloging in Publication Data

Keener, Frederick M   1937–
An essay on Pope.

Includes bibliographical references.
1. Pope, Alexander, 1688–1744. I. Title.
PR3636.K4   821'.5 [B]   74–1260
ISBN 0–231–03827–5

Only where love and need are one,
And the work is play for mortal stakes,
Is the deed ever really done...

                            - ROBERT FROST

Contents

Introduction 1

Part 1   Actions

1   The *Pastorals:* Pamper'd Geese and a Prophecy   19

2   *Windsor-Forest:* Beyond the *Concordia Discors*   30

3   *The Rape of the Lock:* Sublunary Belinda   39

4   *Eloisa to Abelard: Une Lettre Philosophique*   49

5   *An Essay on Man:* To Reason Right Is to Submit   59

6   *Moral Essays:* Against Imitation   70

7   *Imitations of Horace:* Oral Literature   83

8   *The Dunciad, in Four Books:* One Dim Ray of Light   96

Part 2   Acts

9   Transitions   109

10   Toyshop and Boneshop   116

11   The Burden of the Present   128

12   Overtures to Love   135

13   Apocalypse Not Revelation   150

Part 3   Pope's "Proper Character"   157

Postscript   191

Index   193

An Essay on Pope

Introduction

"Criticism in the case of literary figures is never entirely separable from literary history and biography; yet it is more or less separable," writes Maynard Mack in the preface to a masterly recent book.[1] In the more comprehensive twentieth-century books on Alexander Pope—perhaps, indeed, since Samuel Johnson's inimitable *Life*—these elements have never been combined very satisfactorily. During the last several decades no one has even attempted to combine them in any active, total way. The best critics, including Geoffrey Tillotson, Earl R. Wasserman, Aubrey L. Williams, Reuben A. Brower, Thomas R. Edwards, Jr., and Patricia Meyer Spacks, have for the most part circumvented biographical matters.[2] The best biographers (really there is just one,

[1] *The Garden and the City: Retirement and Politics in the Later Poetry of Pope, 1731–1743* (Toronto, 1969), p. vii.

[2] Spacks's *An Argument of Images: The Poetry of Alexander Pope* (Cambridge, Mass., 1971) has some incisive remarks about the effects of Pope's personality on his poems; see esp. pp. 6–7. The chief works of the other critics are cited at appropriate places in my notes, and listed by Cecilia L. Lopez in *Alexander Pope: An Annotated Bibliography, 1945–1967* (Gainesville, 1970). Perhaps the deftest and most ingratiating of books scanning the whole canon, *This Dark Estate: A Reading of Pope* (Perspectives in Criticism, No. 11; Berkeley, 1963), by Thomas R. Edwards, Jr., persuasively describes Pope's development from an Augustan to a grotesque poetic vision, but—as Edwards recognizes (pp. 131–32)—does so with severely limited reference to the poet's historical circumstances.

George Sherburn, although I might mention Robert W. Rogers), perhaps inevitably given the demands of their researches, have practiced criticism with the left hand.[3] A thorough concord of the two disciplines may yet come in our time, since Professor Mack, whose own work has tended to be either critical or biographical, has expressed his hope to produce a "rounded biography."[4] But in the meantime, at least, readers drawn to Pope may find something to interest them in the present, rather angular, interdisciplinary essay, which represents an attempt to read his works and his life together.

Pope studies advance on two levels as well as in the provinces of criticism and biography. Some ten years ago Professor Mack took occasion to assess the twentieth-century "recovery" of the poet, looking forward, since the ice of old prejudices had been broken by a number of good general studies as well as the grand Twickenham Edition, to a time of intensive explication of individual works; very justly he praised Aubrey Williams' investigation of *The Dunciad* and the late Earl Wasserman's commentary on the *Epistle to Bathurst*. The occasion was the publication of Wasserman's edition of that poem (1960)—in a way a curious performance. Not only does Wasserman accord a four-hundred-

---

[3] Sherburn's *The Early Career of Alexander Pope* (Oxford, 1934) ends with the years 1726–27, as (approximately) does Peter Quennell's undistinguished *Alexander Pope: The Education of a Genius, 1688–1728* (New York, 1968). The annual headnotes to Sherburn's edition of *The Correspondence of Alexander Pope* (5 vols.; Oxford, 1956) make a useful complement sketching the later years; helpful too is Robert W. Rogers' *The Major Satires of Alexander Pope* (Illinois Studies in Language and Literature, Vol. 40; Urbana, 1955) and, of course, Maynard Mack's *The Garden and the City*. Both Rogers and Mack tell much about the politics of Pope's later poetry.

[4] *The Garden and the City*, p.viii. John Paul Russo's recent *Alexander Pope: Tradition and Identity* (Cambridge, Mass., 1972), which weaves criticism and biography into a disquisition on Pope's attitude toward fame, may, with the books of Maynard Mack and Patricia Meyer Spacks, signal the beginning of a trend toward more comprehensive study of the poet.

line poem thirty thousand words of concise exegesis, but his commentary becomes conspicuously erudite, even esoteric. Mack foresaw objections: "Some will feel that he has failed to observe the strict test of relevance in some of the learning he deploys, that it contains too many names like Solomon Glassius, Franciscus Collius, Hieremiah Drexelius, and (as Pope might have added) other classics of an age that heard of none."[5] And indeed, anticipating that prediction, Thomas Edwards had complained a few months before that Wasserman's "learning too often leaves the poem behind, as when he finds in Pope's analogy between Blunt and Noah . . . the occasion for a long and rather solemn excursus on the antediluvian sinfulness of man, with references to Athanasius Kircher, Hieremiah Drexelius, J. A. Fabricius, Cornelius a Lapide, and a handful of other exegetes and commentators. The effect is to swamp the poem." These remarks occur in the appendix to an article in which Edwards offered a comparatively secular analysis of the poem (in Wasserman's reading Pope figures as a "lay theologian"[6])—an analysis Edwards defends on sensible, if potentially solipsistic grounds: "If we would bring knowledge to the reading of poetry, as we must, then our obligation is to be tactful, to keep our knowledge always in a servile relation to our human response to what the poem says."[7]

Some interpreters try to bring readers to the poems while others try to bring the poems to readers. At issue is a crucial problem of literary study, that of resolving the different, possibly conflicting claims of fidelity to the historical meaning of a work and of re-

[5] Maynard Mack, review of *Pope's "Epistle to Bathurst": A Critical Reading with An Edition of the Manuscripts*, by Earl R. Wasserman, *Modern Language Notes*, LXXVI (1961), 872.

[6] Earl R. Wasserman, *Pope's "Epistle to Bathurst": A Critical Reading with An Edition of the Manuscripts* (Baltimore, 1960), p. 12.

[7] Thomas R. Edwards, Jr., "'Reconcil'd Extremes': Pope's *Epistle to Bathurst*," *Essays in Criticism*, XI (1961), 308.

sponsiveness to the perceptions and interests of a latter-day reader.[8] This is an aesthetic problem with more important practical consequences than most: it bears hard on the ways past literature shall be approached by teachers and students, for the destination of study cannot be determined without reference to the entrances available. (In its cultural ramifications, the question begins to sound like the matter of space exploration versus urban renewal.) And in Pope studies the question seems urgent just now. As if in harmony with a poet who, in most modern criticism, is more Tory than otherwise, both politically and cosmically, the authors of the best modern commentaries have been much more

[8] E. D. Hirsch, Jr. has emphasized the distinctions between, in his terms, *meaning* and *significance*, and between interpretation and criticism *(Validity in Interpretation* [New Haven, 1967], esp. chapter 2):*meaning* denotes what the author consciously intended to say—and finding out what the author probably intended to say is the purpose of interpretation—while *significance*, a much broader term, denotes what his work says to his reader or readers, whether he probably intended to say it or not. Perceiving significance is the business of criticism, according to Hirsch's distinction. His book, however, concentrates on questions of meaning and interpretation, as has most of the best twentieth-century commentary on Pope—too exclusively, one may think, since like Wit and Judgment in *An Essay on Criticism* interpretation and criticism need each other, and do well to celebrate their anniversaries.

Wesley Morris has thoughtfully surveyed the critical implications of this general problem and a number of American responses to it, in *Towards a New Historicism* (Princeton, 1972). Regarding the problem's cultural ramifications, and the study of Pope, I might say that I have tried to direct this essay toward readers at least somewhat familiar with him and with what has been written about him. Donald B. Clark's introductory *Alexander Pope* (New York, 1967) contains basic information, including historical material about the questions that have occupied commentators. Aware that the "burden of the past" has become a serious problem for writers on Pope, I have tried to achieve a responsible minimum of scholarly documentation, generally attaching my comments to major alternative statements but not marking my every departure from or concurrence with others' views. The best anthology of criticism is *Essential Articles for the Study of Alexander Pope*, ed. Maynard Mack, rev., enl. ed. (Hamden, Conn., 1968).

concerned with relating Pope's work to his time and place and heritage than with relating it to his posterity or with finding some compromise, if possible a conjunction, between the two claims, that of the past and that of the present. When history enters recent Pope criticism, it comes as a variant of historicism: that is, critics place their author squarely and circumstantially in a relation with his predecessors and contemporaries—poets, mythographers, philosophers—but themselves write as if they stood outside time or (the thought is inevitable) as if they had gone back to the time of Pope.

Elegant, aloof, most modern criticism of Pope reads as if it emanated not from twentieth-century America or England but from some miraculously undisturbed eighteenth-century estate, what Hugh Kenner has called "the professional Popeans' Natchez-Augustan manor." [9] Earl Wasserman's purpose, he said, was to read the poems as if he were Pope's "ideal contemporary":[10] the critic becomes a chameleon on the poetry, bringing out color but himself disappearing in the process. Elsewhere, contrasting the antithetical political philosophies of Pope and Sir Robert Walpole in the volatile context of the 1730s, Maynard Mack says we can "appreciate both sides."[11] But if we take history seriously, if through education we have in some degree become constituted as persons by our consciousness of history, I wonder whether we can ever appreciate both sides of a major ideological conflict, no matter how remote it is in time, whether we can really see it as entirely removed from our own historical condition. "All this is comical enough now," Mack says of the opposition to Walpole,

[9] "In the Wake of the Anarch," *Gnomon: Essays on Contemporary Literature* (New York, 1958), p. 176.

[10] *Pope's "Epistle to Bathurst,"* pp. 14–16.

[11] *The Garden and the City,* p. 225.

"as the politics of a past age is always comical if it escapes being tragic,"[12] a pronouncement reminiscent of Strawberry Hill—not, certainly, meant to make us skim the subject but hardly encouraging us to take it seriously. However, the delicacy of the objection I am raising needs emphasis. The problem can be solved with a sword-stroke, as for example in Christopher Caudwell's "Pope perfectly expresses the ideals of the bourgeois class in alliance with a bourgeoisified aristocracy in the epoch of manufacture."[13] The sentence is true to a disturbing degree, but it is also disturbing that Caudwell, more boll weevil than chameleon, has established a historical relation with the poet by obliterating him. One variant of exclusive historicism has simply replaced another, as ideal contemporaneity could be countered by the autobiography of a present-day reader.

The remoteness of Pope, moreover, has been accentuated by the major trend in the last decades of interpretation. T. S. Eliot and other critics of forty years ago, able to taste the marrow in what Matthew Arnold had declared a hollow bone, valued Pope's kind of poetry especially for beginning with the strength of cogent prose. They called it "poetry of statement," although Eliot was careful to say it states "immensely."[14] But since Eliot's time the

[12] Ibid., p. 71.

[13] *Illusion and Reality: A Study of the Sources of Poetry* (New York, 1937), p. 86.

[14] T. S. Eliot, "John Dryden," in *Selected Essays* (New York, [1950]), p. 273. For the term "poetry of statement," see Mark Van Doren's *John Dryden: A Study of His Poetry* (Bloomington, 1946; first published as *The Poetry of John Dryden,* 1920) and K. G. Hamilton's *John Dryden and the Poetry of Statement* (St. Lucia, Queensland, 1967). Hamilton's argument for the oral quality of such poetry (p. 17) connects intriguingly with Johnson's remarks in the *Life of Pope* about the poet's formulaic technique of translating Homer, a surprising anticipation of Milman Parry: "By perpetual practice language had in his mind a systematical arrangement: having always the same use for words, he had words so selected and combined as to be ready at his call" (*Lives of the English Poets,* ed. George Birkbeck Hill [Oxford, 1905], III, 219).

major critical effort has been to emphasize Pope's subtle mythopoetic powers: to stress the connotative elements in the poems,
especially the treasury of allusion. Wasserman—whose tendency
to press analytical techniques more relentlessly than other critics
do accounts for recurrent reference to his positions here, and not
any lack of substance in his admirable if single-minded work on
Pope—in an essay on "The Limits of Allusion in *The Rape of the
Lock*" invited us to "assume . . . it is the nature of Pope's poetry
to incite the reader to search the allusive context for even those
relevances not verbally engaged in his text."[15] Ultimately, almost,
what is in the poem alludes to everything which is not, and a
reader may be encouraged to approach Pope by first reading all
that Pope might have read. Indeed, Wasserman said (impossibly,
like Imlac winding up his euphoric discourse on poetry in
Rasselas) that Pope's poems "consistently ask for a reader who is
equally native to the whole classical-Scriptural world, a Christian
Greco-Roman scrutinizing eighteenth-century culture."[16] Laboratory historicism would simply have readers respond to Pope as
if they were alive two centuries ago, but the allusion-tracing
approach at its extreme seems to require metempsychosis. Or, one
may say, historicism concentrates on what the poem meant in its
time, while allusion-tracing—which may range from a species of
historicism to a springboard of eternal, archetypal meaning—may
seek after either what the poem meant in its time or what it seemingly will always mean. But between quondam meaning and possibly eternal meaning the objects of criticism are not exhausted.
There remains another perspective, that of readers and potential
readers in their own time, inescapably.

How is a given poem distinguishable from the potential whole
of poetry? Metaphorically and allusively, a poem radiates outward,

[15] *Journal of English and Germanic Philology,* LXV (1966), 439.
[16] Ibid., p. 427.

indefinitely if not infinitely. The ripples of allusive poetry like Pope's spread farther and farther, until they seem coextensive with the universe of analogy available to a well-read man of his time, largely the universe of correspondences transmitted to Pope by the Renaissance. Add analogues to sources, as Maynard Mack has done in annotating *An Essay on Man* for the Twickenham Edition, and the universe becomes virtually complete. But in another respect the pull of meaning is centripetal, suggesting in time and space some ratio of statement to implication on which to base relations forward, to posterity, as well as backward. By what concentric system is a poem, or a group of poems, or the whole canon of a poet, contained so as not to explode, so as not to mean nothing by meaning everything?—and so as to mean something in relation to its historical origins that remains significant because readers perceive connections between an old poet's place in history and their own. If we are fully to understand and feel the presence of a poet, we must make an effort to dispel as well as to preserve his "pastness," to enclose ourselves within him and him within us, to see him from inside and from outside, to look at him within and against both our time and his.

Such are the connections sought in this book, connections so extensive that the book must remain an essay. Commonly, academic treatment of an author stands, or ought to stand, foursquare on the history of the archeology performed to date. Impersonal excavation of Alexander Pope's remains goes forward in various quarters, toward a still remote Baconian millennium of objective synthesis. Historicist research uncovers new strata of meaning year by year, disjunctively and diffusively numbering new gems and shards, to be labeled and evaluated from various points of view according to the varying sets of unspoken values which motivate the work of recovery. And the merit of the work can hardly be questioned, so successful has the effort been to reclaim

Pope in multifaceted actuality from the genteel impressionism and paternalistic moralism that passed for critical judgment in some persuasive nineteenth-century mouths. Still, my approach to Pope is different from (although at every turn it has been facilitated by) those approaches typical of contemporary Popeans. A too-exclusive attention has been paid to backgrounds in the best criticism, to Pope's relation with traditions of antiquity and especially of the Renaissance. In contrast, I have emphasized his affinities with the Enlightenment, an aspect of his work bound to be given more weight in coming years. My main purpose, however, has been to suggest an alternative to the disjunctiveness and diffusiveness, and particularly to the implicit antiquarianism, now dominant in Pope studies. This essay is primarily the record of an attempt to perceive coherence and development both accessible and engaging in the works and other records of a poet too easily regardable as wholly alien from that posterity he so wished to please. Relying, as an essayist may, on my own responses to the poems, trying to foreshorten the distance that separates Alexander Pope from us, I have sought basic denominators of his works and also of his life, probing in each for centers from which the details radiate, for handles enabling a reader to carry poems and poet away with him.

My essay is in three parts, and the first part concentrates on— what a reader begins with—Pope's major poems. Where present, the most obviously unifying and accessible element of literature seems to be simply the fiction or story, in E. M. Forster's language that "low atavistic" element. [17] With the story, explicit or implicit (to put the matter too simply for the moment), I have begun again and again; not, I think, an approach that would have displeased Alexander Pope. "We care not to Study, or to Anatomize a Poem, but only to read it for our entertainment," said Pope in a letter to

[17] *Aspects of the Novel* (London, 1949), p. 27.

Bolingbroke, [18] a sentiment emphasizing the poet's distance from us in several ways that need no explanation. To judge by what he wrote *about* poems, he did not closely analyze them; like Swift and other kindred spirits of his time, he distrusted anatomy of anything, fearful of the literalism that kills life, and he satirized such insensitivity on many occasions. Yet though reticent about his own poetical projects, he nevertheless supplied arguments for *An Essay on Criticism, Eloisa to Abelard, An Essay on Man,* the *Moral Essays,* and *The Dunciad,* and in a conversation with Joseph Spence he described what he called the three "tours" of poetry: the "design," the language, the versification—then added a fourth, the "'expression,' or manner of painting the humours, characters, and things that fall in with your design."[19] The design is basic, and basic to the design, at least in narrative poetry, is the "fable" or "the main Story . . ., *the Return of Ulysses,* the *Settlement of the* Trojans *in* Italy, or the like. That of the *Iliad* is *the Anger of* Achilles."[20] Following French Aristotelians of the later seventeenth century, Pope begins formal analysis of epics, whether in his earnest remarks on Homer or in the recipe he provides in the *Peri Bathous* (which "though written in so ludicrous a way," he said, "may be very well worth reading seriously as an art of rhetoric"[21])—begins by attending to the fable and its action or plot. Yet his analysis seldom proceeds far, perhaps in part because he recognized, like the readers of much modern criticism, and like Freud, that analysis may prove interminable; or perhaps because he lacked the stomach for sustained dissection. There persists in

[18] *The Correspondence of Alexander Pope,* ed. George Sherburn (Oxford, 1956), II, 228.

[19] Joseph Spence, *Observations, Anecdotes, and Characters of Books and Men Collected from Conversation,* ed. James M. Osborn (2 vols.; Oxford, 1966), I, 167.

[20] "Preface," *The Iliad of Homer,* ed. Maynard Mack, Vol. VII of the Twickenham Edition (London, 1967), p. 5.

[21] Spence, I, 57.

Pope criticism a complementary undertone suggesting that, the poet being a miniaturist in so many ways, he was best in couplets and worst at whole poems, preoccupied with incidental effects, at something of a loss in large designing.[22] More work certainly needs to be done on this point.

Through much of Part I, when approaching Pope's poems — and indeed, later when describing Pope's career as well—I concern myself with total designs and particularly with fables, acts, and actions. Simply asking what is happening in Pope's poems, and why, a reader is sometimes surprised to find the answer less evident than he would suppose. He finds gaps in the chain of events. How, for example, did the earthly lover gain entry to Belinda's heart, and how, at the end, does the lock rise into the sky? What movement is there beneath the exquisite amber surface of the *Pastorals?* Why does Father Thames enter *Windsor-Forest?* What is the final disposition of Eloisa's mind? Why may the four so-called *Moral Essays* stand in their present order? These and other questions, as yet not fully answered, will certainly pique the curiosity of anyone receptive to Pope whether my answers seem adequate or not. Such questions usefully point toward one term in that centripetal relation, that ratio of statement to implica-

---

[22] In a fairly recent instance, Irvin Ehrenpreis—before attempting to describe the coherence of the *Epistle to a Lady*—comments, "Few of Pope's works pretend to exhibit throughout the sort of design which his couplets and his verse paragraphs possess" ("The Cistern and the Fountain: Art and Reality in Pope and Gray," in *Studies in Criticism and Aesthetics: Essays in Honor of Samuel Holt Monk*, ed. Howard Anderson and John S. Shea [Minneapolis, 1967], p. 158). Reuben A. Brower begins *Alexander Pope: The Poetry of Allusion* (Oxford, 1959) by declaring that his "first and last concern is with the poems, with their poetic character and design" (p. vii), yet as Hoyt Trowbridge observed in a review, Brower's sensitivity to shifting, allusive poetic tones seems to distract him from "continuous and sequential" aspects of design such as plot and action, e.g., the "distinguishable complication, climax, and resolution" of *Eloisa to Abelard* (*Philological Quarterly*, XL [1961], 414–16).

tion, which brings focus to consideration of the poems, whatever the context.[23]

Moreover, such questions draw attention to the character of the narrator or speaker of the poems, whose voice joins the parts even when a fictional or argumentative link seems to be missing, and whose speech, from poem to poem through Pope's canon from beginning to end, will, when traced, reveal a remarkable series of changes in his implied character and personality, an arc of development toward attitudes more congenial to present-day readers than what historicism, and especially allusion-tracing, can discover. But even apart from the congeniality of Pope's later attitudes, the arc of his development is itself engaging. Generally speaking, the design of the later poems differs strikingly from that of the earlier, as the poet increasingly makes himself his subject, whereas he had before seemed to take himself for granted, had readily assumed standard poetic guises. As his representation of himself changes, he depends less on external "design," on plot or argument, and more on internal associations. He adopts new poetical standpoints to adapt his art, and presumably himself, to new historical conditions. To confine one's view to the distant retrospective relations that are the historicists' stock in trade is therefore to attempt to make the poet's springs run backward, to read him against the current of his development. In effect it is to read him as his predecessors would. We must read him as ourselves; our reading, though, as much as that of the historicist, is primarily

---

[23] "A poetry of statement will be signalized not by the absence of metaphorical effects but by their use in such a way that they do not disturb a logical surface of statement" (Maynard Mack, "'Wit and Poetry and Pope': Some Observations on His Imagery," in *Pope and His Contemporaries: Essays Presented to George Sherburn*, ed. James L. Clifford and Louis A. Landa [Oxford, 1949], p. 21). This is a very useful general comment. I would add to it the observation that in Pope's finest poems, *The Rape of the Lock* for example, breaks in the chain of statement necessitate the critical search for metaphorical links, locatable in what might be called the "lower sky" of implication.

critical, not biographical, except in its giving weight to the fact that all the poems were written by the same person, and to the likelihood that changes across the canon have critical significance. It proceeds from the poems initially, not from what other sources tell about the poet. And indeed it aspires to being especially, fully critical because, from what it acknowledges as its necessary vantage point, that of the present, it attempts to comprehend its subject's subsequent as well as prior relations, the fullness of his meaning and interest to us.

Part II of this essay extends the investigation undertaken in Part I by bringing together the changes in Pope's poetic voice and relating them to the events of his life as we know about it from sources other than his poems. Pope's personae seek a complement in what can be gathered about the person behind them. The hazards and limitations of such a project can scarcely be overestimated; indeed, to some scholars the attempt will seem indefensible. Recent studies have emphasized the artifice in Pope's self-portrayal, have valuably concentrated on description of Pope's persona or personae. As Samuel Johnson shrewdly remarked, "Are we to think Pope was happy, because he says so in his writings? We see in his writings what he wished the state of his mind to appear."[24] The gap between dead Pope and his living

[24] James Boswell, *Life of Johnson*, ed. George Birkbeck Hill, rev. and enl. by L. F. Powell, III (Oxford, 1934), 251. Less waspishly, but no less shrewdly, John Butt penetrated to the heart of the question when he asked, how might Pope's works be said to reveal "the real man? Professor Maynard Mack, in an essay called 'The Muse of Satire' [*Yale Review*, XLI (1951), 80–92], has shown how closely modelled the poet's *persona* is upon the traditional figure of the satirist. Yet at the same time it is possible to annotate each incident from the satires and show its derivation from the poet's own biography. We are presented with a peculiar blending of the artifact and the real, one of the strangest confusions of life and letters. So accustomed had he become to this blend that Pope himself may not have known how precisely to distinguish the historical portrait from the literary one. That is the enigma that a study of his life and writings offers" ("Pope: The Man and the Poet," in *Of Books and Humankind: Essays and Poems Presented to Bonamy Dobrée*, ed. John Butt [London, 1965], p. 79).

pages is ultimately unbridgeable. But such rigorous thinking, with
its Humean unanswerableness, seems itself finally valuable only
for its cautionary effects—and may be disastrous for practical
comprehension of the poet. We must work with Pope's personae
just as we do with our acquaintances', filling the chinks with
poor, paltry, indispensable speculation, if we are to begin to
grasp what Pope in *An Essay on Criticism* called a "proper Character" of the poet, "His Fable, Subject, Scope in ev'ry Page,/
Religion, Country, Genius of his Age." To synthesize Pope's
characteristics, as it were from the inside, I have posited responsiveness on his part to the social and political conditions of
his time, drawn rather broadly. In this effort—which takes me
uncomfortably outside the limits of my formal training—I have
depended to some extent upon Erik Erikson's psychological
biographies, especially *Young Man Luther*, and Isaac Kramnick's
provocative work on the politics of the early eighteenth century. [25]
Attempting to unite discretion with zest, I have sought brevity
almost above all, constructing something like a DNA model of
the poet instead of a full reproduction; and I have not scrutinized
his paper-saving habits or attempted to read the implications
of that baleful day when, as a child, Pope was trampled by an
angry cow.

Art and life being different things, they cannot be thoroughly,
exactly joined. Yet being related, they should not, in fact cannot,
be kept separate from each other. Anyone who knows anything
about Pope's life will not—in practice, simply cannot—regard
Pope as a mere voice or persona. For minute critical purposes,
for analysis of specific works, information about the poet derived
from outside the poems may be deliberately disregarded, with

[25] *Bolingbroke and His Circle: The Politics of Nostalgia in the Age of Walpole* (Cambridge, Mass., 1968).

profitable results. But only temporarily. The analysis performed, the critic proofreads his typescript and then readmits to his mind that image, that complex of memories and imaginings which he calls "Pope." His Pope, whether the critic realizes it or not, is part of the critic's being, related to everything in his life: his sense of art and life and history (the list expands infinitely), of Pope's identity and of his own, of everything linking and separating these things. To describe the relations perfectly is impossible; the very impossibility, however, keeps the humanities going, assures them of a future, for the relations may be described to an increasing extent, to our increased satisfaction.

"The more perfect the artist, the more completely separate in him will be the man who suffers and the mind which creates," wrote T. S. Eliot in an essay underlying modern disjunctive approaches to literary study, "impersonalist" approaches (to borrow Eliot's label).[26] Eliot did have a point: it is the poet's poems, and especially their merit as poems, that command our attention as readers. But that is just the beginning of a process where the critic is concerned. The more perfect the critic, the more he will take not just the poems but everything, and the relations of everything, into account. If it is known, for example, that the poet suffered—if it is known, at least in part, how he suffered, what he suffered—then such knowledge makes its mark, indelibly, on the reader and has to influence his critical response, although traces of that particular influence may be excluded from his written criticism. Whether such matters should be excluded, however, is a real, disturbing question. What is gained in precision may partially be lost in other ways.

The matter of precision remains very important: we read

[26] "Tradition and the Individual Talent," *Selected Essays* (New York, [1950]), pp. 7–8, 11.

literature and criticism to clarify our perceptions and feelings, among other reasons. An artist or critic may be superb in this respect alone, teaching us to see and feel, no matter what he does besides this; this he has to do, whatever he does. But we want him to do more. When we read, we are looking in the words for someone for whom we can feel affection. We are pleased, when we expect just an author, to find a man or woman. Dante, in our minds if not in our explications, is, among other things, a political exile, and that he was really an exile is related to our deepest response to the cumulative persona of his works; the historical fact and our response to it are necessarily factors of whatever feeling we have for his writing. If we continue to read Dante, and if we do so for fully human reasons, we go back to him not just because we admire his artistry but because we sympathize with him in the totality of our knowledge of him. As human beings we need finally to base our deepest appreciation of literature upon just such sympathy—by which I mean not pity, although pity will sometimes enter in, but something more general, shared feeling. We see and feel something in Dante, or in Pope, which we recognize in ourselves, which reading the poet and reading about him help us to comprehend, to enjoy, or to bear. If what I am saying is not so, then oddly enough poetry must be read with—what even Eliot condemned in many poets—a "dissociated sensibility." Even if that *is* the way we should read it, however, as human beings we cannot.

Hence, despite the conquests of division achieved by modern commentators on Pope, and according their accomplishments all due praise, a student will feel his blood quicken when he turns from them back to a critical biography of the poet like Samuel Johnson's in *The Lives of the Poets*. Johnson saw Pope somewhat unsteadily by modern standards, but he did see him whole, and the *Life* lives as a result of Johnson's vigorous attempt to read the poems and the poet with an eye to all significant relations.

As pairs will, the two main parts of the present essay have suggested the need for a third in which, taking my departure from Johnson's version of Pope's "proper Character," I sum up mine and turn to several concluding points about its bearing on the poems and about their relation to living readers. Still close to Pope in time and joined to him by many strands of shared sensibility, Johnson defended him with the ringing challenge "If Pope be not a poet, where is poetry to be found?" Now, so far removed from Pope, the distance seemingly so often increased by impersonal, historicist analysis of the poems, we might rephrase the question, but quietly, not at all rhetorically. If the poet be not Pope, where is Pope to be found?

Part 1. Actions

---

1. The *Pastorals*: Pamper'd Geese and a Prophecy

Pope's are the last real pastorals written in English. They are the last, that is, to which the poet could seriously hope reality might attach itself as it had to equivalent poems by Spenser and Milton, Virgil, and the ancients. Pope's are the last pastorals we have wherein Renaissance myth and convention may not seem patently unnatural. Yet the age to which the young poet offered his careful series was one of ascendant realism in philosophy and literature, was increasingly an age attentive to facts of experience and wary of illusion[1]—an age, it would seem, particularly inhospitable to pastorals. The peculiar condition of the shepherds Pope created in such circumstances may speak to us if we peer past the glossy surface of the poems.

"Perhaps their loves, or else their sheep,/ Was all that did their silly thoughts so busy keep." According to the Twickenham editors, Pope's *Pastorals* yield a vision of "an ordered world . . .

---

[1] For an informative account of the early eighteenth-century climate of opinion as it relates to philosophical and literary realism, see Ian Watt's *The Rise of the Novel: Studies in Defoe, Richardson and Fielding* (London, 1957), esp. chapter 1.

which answers to man's needs,"[2] a comment consistent enough
with Pope's own opinion of the form as delivered in his prefatory
"Discourse on *Pastoral.*" Classically, as Pope says, such verse
represents "the Golden age" (ll. 39–40) when in song the first
shepherds "took occasion to celebrate their own felicity. From
hence a Poem was invented, and afterwards improv'd to a perfect
image of that happy time" (ll. 18–20). "We must therefore use
some illusion to render a Pastoral delightful; and this consists in
exposing the best side only of a shepherd's life, and in concealing
its miseries" (ll. 63–65). The trouble is, these comments authorial
and editorial seem more applicable to the history of the pastoral
before Pope than to the four poems Pope wrote. His particular
shepherds show a constant disposition to find that nature sympa-
thizes with them and will submit to their wishes; but nature,
either hostile or indifferent, in general walks its seasonal round
without concern for the shepherds' feelings.

Who submits to whom is clear in *Spring:* the swains follow
nature. After Daphnis asks, "Why sit we mute, when early Linnets
sing,/ When warbling *Philomel* salutes the Spring?" (ll. 25–26),
Strephon suggests a singing contest. Competition and a desire to
put themselves in harmony with the warblers—which, by contrast, have begun to sing of their own accord, without external
incentives—move the shepherds to lift their voices. In the course
of his song, Strephon describes Delia's alleged power over nature:

> All Nature mourns, the Skies relent in Show'rs,
> Hush'd are the Birds, and clos'd the drooping Flow'rs;

[2] E. Audra and Aubrey Williams, eds., *Pastoral Poetry and An Essay on Criticism,*
Vol. I of the Twickenham Edition (London, 1961), p. 53. In various passages
introductory to the *Pastorals,* the editors seem troubled by the incongruous behavior of Pope's shepherds (see especially p. 45, regarding the "self-absorption" of
Alexis in *Summer*), a trait important to the present essay.

> If *Delia* smile, the Flow'rs begin to spring,
> The Skies to brighten, and the Birds to sing.   (ll. 69–72)

Does the linnet pause to listen while Stephon sings, do blossoms bend toward him? In other words, does nature support, does the narrator sanction, Strephon's indulgence in the pathetic fallacy? No, at the end of the contest it begins to rain, unsolicited. To be sure, the showers will bring flowers, or so the narrator Damon observes, finding a convenient consolation; and certainly the dominant of the first pastoral is in a warm major key, but it is so for the last time in the series.

Of the four poems, it must be noted, only the first three have narrators, witnesses to the effects of the characters' pleas and predictions. In only one place does the witness make an unreserved attempt to corroborate the shepherds' faith in nature's personal responsiveness:

> Soft as he mourn'd, the Streams forgot to flow,
> The Flocks around a dumb Compassion show,
> The *Naiads* wept in ev'ry Watry Bow'r,
> And *Jove* consented in a silent Show'r.   (*Summer*, ll. 5–8)

But the attempt at corroboration lacks force, since in this pastoral it is hard to tell where the narrator stops speaking and the character begins. Elsewhere, characters never give such evidence; in fact, what Alexis goes on to say about his environment in *Summer* is totally at variance with the lines just quoted. At another place, later, as the notes variorum of the Twickenham Edition show, Pope expunged a narrative line of this kind: "To whose Complaints the list'ning Forests bend" (*Autumn*, 1, 3). For the most part he let the characters' speeches stand on their own merits (rather shakily, a reader may feel), and in the last of the series, the gravest, two shepherds speak an unmediated, unframed dialogue, quite alone, indeed forlorn. It would be gratuitous to infer that the shepherds' sorrow has distressed the narrator enough to drive him away, as if he feared that they would next, impossibly, turn to him for help; but that this odd thought could arise may tellingly suggest the quality of tentativeness in Pope's approach to the pastoral. It is as if he wanted to dip himself in the genre but did not mean to get wet. *The Shepherd's Week* of his friend John Gay, published five years later, contains lines such as "The rolling Streams with watry Grief shall flow,/ And Winds shall moan aloud—when loud they blow" (*Friday*, ll. 35–36), lines Pope's narrator might conceivably speak were he less controlled.

Alexis, the major figure of *Summer*, cannot begin to feel at home in nature, for amid the torrid heat and drought of the dog days he is all at odds with himself, pining away with love for an unnamed girl whose unseasonable heart holds eternal winter (l. 22). "Once I was skill'd in ev'ry Herb that grew,/ And ev'ry Plant that drinks the Morning Dew" (ll. 31–32). But no more; he has lost the salutary intimacy he once enjoyed with the plants. He has become a misfit in Arcadian Windsor Forest, viewing his misery from the inside and expressing it in first-person plaints, seeing himself from the outside and venting bewilderment in third-person exclamations: "Ah wretched Shepherd, what avails thy Art,/ To cure thy Lambs, but not to heal thy Heart!" (ll. 33–34). Literally beside himself, he is fully sensible of the division between what he is and what he was and ought to be.

Like Milton's Satan he has brought Hell into Paradise: "This harmless Grove no lurking Viper hides,/ But in my Breast the Serpent Love abides" (ll. 67–68). Like Strephon, in *Spring*, he speaks of nature's solicitude, prophesying that "Where-e're you walk, cool Gales shall fan the Glade" (l. 73). Would they? The question is not answered. Alexis' beloved never arrives, and his musings cease when he notices the other shepherds moving off to

shelter themselves from the burning noon. There is no respite for
him, however, scorched by a fever which no grove can relieve; the
sun will set, but not Alexis' agony (that insomnia also plagues the
shepherds we learned at the beginning of *Spring*). In the last lines
Alexis cries, "On me Love's fiercer Flames for ever prey,/ By
Night he scorches, as he burns by Day," lines begging for comparison with the prototype of *Summer*, Virgil's second *Eclogue*. There
too a lover pines for his beloved—there it is the beloved who is
named Alexis—and closes his lament much as Pope's Alexis does.
In Dryden's translation,

> Cool breezes now the raging heats remove:
> Ah, cruel Heaven, that made no cure for love!
> I wish for balmy sleep, but wish in vain;
> Love has no bounds in pleasure, or in pain.

But unlike Pope's poem, Virgil's does not end at this point. The
narrator reenters to speak the last lines, in the course of which
he dashes some cold common sense on the overheated lover:

> What frenzy, shepherd, has thy soul possess'd?
> Thy vineyard lies half prun'd, and half undress'd.
> Quench, Corydon, thy long unanswer'd fire;
> Mind what the common wants of life require:
> On willow twigs employ thy weaving care,
> And find an easier love, tho' not so fair.

For one reason or another, Pope's narrator hangs back, holding his
tongue, intensifying our impression of Alexis' desolation.

In *Autumn* the series plunges into deeper gloom as AEgon
mourns a "faithless," Hylas "an absent Love"—Hylas who, one
reads, could teach "Rocks to weep, and made the *Mountains* groan"
(l. 16). Here, if the narrator may be trusted, is the sort of miracle-
worker Windsor desperately needs, and Hylas proves the first to
sing, his performance a string of analogies bound with joy:

> Thro' Rocks and Caves the Name of *Delia* sounds,
> *Delia,* each Cave and ecchoing Rock rebounds.
> Ye Pow'rs, what pleasing Frensie sooths my Mind!
> Do Lovers dream, or is my *Delia* kind?
> She comes, my *Delia* comes!—now cease my Lay,
> And cease ye Gales to bear my Sighs away!
> Next AEgon sung, while Windsor Groves admired. . . . (ll. 49–55)

Happy Hylas; but AEgon's strains recall Alexis' in *Summer,* bitter words of alienation and despair voiced with woeful iteration almost to the end of the poem. There the narrator speaks once more, in fact speaks for the last time in the series, yet what he says is puzzling, as if his attention had wandered from what the shepherds have been saying. AEgon's song concludes:

> One Leap from yonder Cliff shall end my Pains.
> No more ye Hills, no more resound my Strains!
>   Thus sung the Shepherds till th' Approach of Night,
> The Skies yet blushing with departing Light,
> When falling Dews with Spangles deck'd the Glade,
> And the low Sun had lengthen'd ev'ry Shade.   (ll. 95–100)

One wonders: did AEgon jump, or was the mere thought of jumping sufficient to abate his misery? Was Hylas' Delia really approaching, or did Hylas merely experience the fantasy of a "pleasing Frensie"?—a "false surmise," the pastoral equivalent of King Lear's thinking Cordelia was still breathing. A final question: were the rocks really docile, the hills resonant with sympathy? Far from it: the light of day fades slowly, radiantly, obliviously; the glade glistens while the shepherds prepare for another uneasy night.

   Still worse, with the coming of *Winter* the bane of death succeeds trials of absence and betrayal as Lycidas bids Thyrsis commemorate Daphne's passing. Moreover, the first two lines indicate that Thyrsis is being asked precisely because nature does not provide a suitably lugubrious song: "*Thyrsis,* the Musick of that murm'ring Spring/ Is not so mournful as the Strains you sing." Nature seems unconcerned about Daphne. Among terrestrial beings only the shepherds, as usual, are awake:

> Now sleeping Flocks on their soft Fleeces lye,
> The Moon, serene in Glory, mounts the Sky,
> While silent Birds forget their tuneful Lays. . . .   (ll. 5–7)

Mainly a long epitaph, Thyrsis' song instructs nature to "change" (l. 27). "'Tis done," he remarks two lines later in one of literature's more expeditious metamorphoses; but now perhaps *I* have become as unsympathetic as everything else, though in self-justification I may point out that as early as lines 9–10 Thyrsis had reported frost in the leafless, beautyless groves. The change: depredations of winter; the reason: Daphne's death. As for her, like the moon she "mounts on high,/ Above the clouds" to experience "Eternal Beauties," pick "unfading Flow'rs" (ll. 69–74). In short, stepmother nature in her seasonal decay has proven no more solicitous of mankind than she has throughout the other pastorals; a shepherd's lot is not at all easy: to be rained on, scorched, tormented, sleepless, betrayed, reft and bereft. In the final lines of *Winter* Thyrsis understandably contemplates escape from this world of "unwholesome Dews" and "noxious Shade" where mankind quails before the northern blast. It is dead Daphne who has found a truly golden age beyond time.

Yet, and significantly, Thyrsis is trying to thrust his own melancholy upon nature, as the comments of his companion, both early and late, quite clearly show. At the beginning of the poem Lycidas had anticipated the "kind rains" of another spring and the "future Harvest of the field" (ll. 15–16); at the end, having no plans of his own for departure, he looks forward to making a sacrifice of spring lamb for newly promoted Daphne. A singular shepherd he, for despite Pope's description of *pastoral* in the "Discourse" the herdsmen, on the whole, are a maladjusted lot, and the *Pastorals,* despite the interpretations of both swains and editors, manifestly do not represent a congenial world such as that conjured up by Marlowe's Passionate Shepherd. Urging the rolling year, Pope renders winter as well as spring, and the spring which follows winter—a world where birds do not sing madrigals but men persist in believing birds do. In *An Essay on Man* the poet would provide several lines not inapplicable to his high-strung swains, the lines about the goose destined for *pâté,* who thought the universe, or at least mankind, had been created to cram him full (III. 45–46). If we have been shown the "best side only of a shepherd's life," who would want to witness the worst! If this was the Golden Age, what must succeeding eras have been like?

But perhaps, as Pope claimed in concluding *Guardian* No. 40, comparing his four poems triumphantly with rustic Ambrose Philips', "they are by no means *Pastorals,* but *something better.*" That is, although I have emphasized elements in Pope's verse which have generally escaped comment, perhaps they have nevertheless been felt. It would be difficult, I think, to read the *Pastorals* without feeling some degree of—not necessarily disappointment but unfulfillment, whether or not one had built high hopes on Pope's remarks in the "Discourse"; for the swains prove sillier than they need have been, and sadder. Certainly a reader finds more variety, mainly through infusions of joy, in Theocritus, Virgil, and Spenser—in Theocritus' famous idyll concerning the harvest festival (VII), for example, not that it alone contains such happiness, or Virgil's messianic eclogue, the fourth.[3] Hence it

---

[3] Comparison with Virgil ought to be pressed further here, not simply to the general observation that his collection is more miscellaneous and more cheerful on the whole than Pope's, nor to remarking (as I have in my text) the difference between Pope's *Summer* and Eclogue II, but also at least as far as citation of the contrast between *Autumn* and Eclogue VIII, its prototype. In Virgil the second of the two speakers, not (as in Pope) the first, thinks he sees his beloved returning to him, while the first speaker is the one who meditates suicide. In Pope the worse situation is climactic, not in Virgil.

may be appropriate to mention a curious statement Pope made to Joseph Spence, that the "last" pastoral was the poet's own favorite, referring not to *Winter* but to *Messiah*, published three years after the *Pastorals*, in 1712.[4] For *Messiah*, that flamboyant conflation of the fourth *Eclogue* and Isaiah, in several ways does continue and complete the *Pastorals*.

Most obviously, it presents an indisputably golden age replete with a felicity so strikingly absent from the earlier poems. *Messiah* does begin by promising to outdo them:

> Ye Nymphs of *Solyma!* begin the Song:
> To heav'nly Themes sublimer Strains belong.
> The Mossie Fountains and the Sylvan Shades,
> The Dreams of *Pindus* and th' Aonian *Maids*,
> Delight no more. . . .

And certain physical, implicitly spiritual benefits to be wrought by the Messiah—"From Storms a Shelter, and from Heat a Shade" (l. 16)—would have found grateful recipients in such sufferers as the *Pastorals* depict; "No sigh, no Murmur the wide World shall hear,/ From ev'ry Face he wipes off ev'ry Tear"; He shall bind Death in chains (ll. 45–47). Moreover, if the miseries concealed, according to Pope's "Discourse," in conventional pastorals are the day-to-day tasks pertinent to the shepherd's life ("Why, we are

---

[4] Joseph Spence, *Observations, Anecdotes, and Characters of Books and Men Collected from Conversation*, ed. James M. Osborn (2 vols.; Oxford, 1966), I, 175. According to Osborn, it is questionable whether—but not impossible that—Spence interpreted Pope correctly. The Twickenham editors see *Messiah* as distinctly separate from the *Pastorals* (though it was grouped with them in Pope's *Works* of 1717) for reasons suspiciously including an unironic reading of a comment in *Guardian* No. 40: that "the Criticks in general" had refused to classify the fourth *Eclogue* as a true pastoral (I, 100–101); the critics, Pope says there, will allow only two of the ten *Eclogues* to be true pastoral!—not the only apparent absurdity in Pope's passage. The *Pastorals* are linked with *Messiah*, as well as with the Renaissance tradition of the genre, in a valuable commentary by Martin C. Battestin, "The Transforming Power: Nature and Art in Pope's Pastorals," *Eighteenth-Century Studies*, II (1969), 183–204.

still handling our ewes, and their fells you know are greasy,"
observes Corin in *As You Like It*, iii.ii.50–51), there is more
technical information in *Messiah*, in the description of the Good
Shepherd (ll. 49–54), than may be found in all four *Pastorals* put
together. The mystical poem has a reality about it that the toy
Pastorals want.

Most to the point, however, *Messiah* describes a time when
nature shall no longer be indifferent to man, or to Man. The
attentiveness hyperbolically promised by Alexis in *Summer:* "The
wondring Forests soon shou'd dance again" (l. 82), to cite but one
line among many—that solicitude, never realized except in imagination by the shepherds, in *Messiah* comes true, becomes visible:

> See Nature hasts her earliest Wreaths to bring,
> With all the Incense of the breathing Spring:
> See lofty *Lebanon* his Head advance,
> See nodding Forests on the Mountains dance,
> See spicy Clouds from lowly *Saron* rise,
> And *Carmel's* flow'ry Top perfumes the Skies!   (ll. 23–28)

This Man may justly say, in the words of the *Essay*, "See all things
for my use!" (iii.45). The pathetic fallacy in this case, and this
case alone, becomes no longer fallacious. No wonder the swain in
the desert shall "with surprise/ See Lillies spring, and sudden
Verdure rise" (ll. 67–68), considering his own sorry experience of
the past.

Pope's shepherds inhabit Windsor Forest at an unspecified or
ambiguous time; they are primitive Sicilians, as their names indicate, yet the first three pastorals are addressed to various of Pope's
contemporaries, so that a reader must place them both b.c. and
a.d. A like form of superimposition seems evident in *Messiah*.
Blending Old Testament references with New (for example, the
Good Shepherd of John 10:11), the eighteenth-century poet can

be both Isaiah and himself by predicting Christ's birth as if it were
the Second Coming, a strategy employed throughout the latter
part of the poem, which harmoniously confuses birth and death
and resurrection—

> See future Sons, and Daughters yet unborn
> In crowding Ranks on ev'ry Side arise,
> Demanding Life, impatient for the Skies!   (ll. 88–90)

—eclipsing night and day and the seasons, those intervals so
nicely demarcated in the *Pastorals*, by an effulgence of eternal light
that does away with the mundane things from which the poor
pagan shepherds once sought sympathy—a bursting of earth's
restraints here very effectively realized in the enjambment of
"shine Reveal'd":

> See Heav'n its sparkling Portals wide display,
> And break upon thee in a Flood of Day!
> No more the rising *Sun* shall gild the Morn,
> Nor Evening *Cynthia* fill her silver Horn,
> But lost, dissolv'd in thy superior Rays;
> One Tyde of Glory, one unclouded Blaze,
> O'erflow thy Courts: The LIGHT HIMSELF shall shine
> Reveal'd; and *God*'s eternal Day be thine!
> The Seas shall waste; the Skies in Smoke decay;
> Rocks fall to Dust, and Mountains melt away;
> But fix'd *His* Word, *His* saving Pow'r remains:
> Thy Realm for ever lasts! thy own *Messiah* reigns!   (ll. 97–108)

The golden age glimpsed in the Elysium of the fourth pastoral
comes to the living in the fifth. Here, finally, remote as it may
seem—totally elsewhere—is a world which Pope's earliest public
speaker can really sing about. As we shall see, visions of such
other worlds haunt most of his earlier poetry.

2. *Windsor-Forest*: Beyond the Concordia Discors

Pope's poem of 1713 celebrating the Treaty of Utrecht, its Tory proponents, Queen Anne, and much else has been studied with splendid erudition for the way it illuminates the political theory and cosmic metaphor of *concordia discors*.[1] Where there was once dreadful tyranny, in the forests of England, all Britain, and much of the world, the queen has established a fine, dynamic equipoise of conflicting interests that is divine order, yet full of human energy. Now the Peace of Utrecht lays a basis for international harmony, prompting Father Thames himself to surface at the end of the poem and to prophesy a new golden age when

[1] Earl R. Wasserman, *The Subtler Language* (Baltimore, 1959), pp. 101–68. The concept of harmonious confusion is a little confusing itself, since the harmonized elements may be understood as either (a) contrary to one another or (b) simply different from one another; that is, either at strife or merely varied. Pope's preliminary exposition of the concept admits both meanings (ll. 11–16), and Professor Wasserman, though he incidentally makes the distinction (p. 142), might have drawn it more sharply and extensively. According to my reading of the poem's final vision, mankind will one day achieve a condition in which all contrariety is spent and only variety remains, as seas will "but join the Regions they divide" (l. 400).

England shall have taught all the world to replace destructive
strife with salutary competition, when commerce and prosperity
shall supplant warfare. The inevitable strife of humanity shall be
then more harmonious than ever before.

Put thus baldly, Pope's argument seems so Rotarian that one
might wish the poem ended otherwise—as, indeed, I think it does.
The final vision, I shall argue, is of a *concordia*, and furthermore,
the text indicates that realization of the vision is attainable by
Pope's contemporaries, at least realizable by them as individ-
uals.

Just past the middle of the poem comes a passage originating in
patriotism:

> Happy the Man whom this bright Court approves,
> His Sov'reign favours, and his Country loves;
> Happy next him who to these Shades retires,
> Whom Nature charms, and whom the Muse inspires,
> Whom humbler Joys of home-felt Quiet please,
> Successive Study, Exercise and Ease.   (ll. 235–40)

Confusing lines: who is happier, the courtier or the muse-inspired
man enjoying Horatian retirement? A man like Lord Lansdowne,
the Granville mentioned at various emphatic places in the poem, a
peer and a minister enabled by his office to take an active part in
ordering world affairs—or a man like Pope himself, tranquilly
busy with his own pursuits while others hunt in Windsor Forest.
Taken together the lines give supreme happiness to the courtier,
the parallel ellipses suggesting *happy is the man, happy next him is he.*
But to be sure, this is an awkwardly incremental sequence, and
surely avoidable; Pope might have written, certainly could have
conceived, "Happy next he" if he sought unequivocal clarity.

Perhaps he did not; the ambiguity is suggestive.[2] Although a poet
praising a triumph of diplomacy cannot at the same time question
the statesman's self-esteem, he may have—and hint—doubts
about its degree of validity, especially to make a point of more
than occasional significance. Somewhat comparably, the poet of
the *Georgics* and the *Aeneid* glorified Rome without forgetting the
tears her achievements had cost, the cruelty. Augustus' Virgil,
the Pope Granville commanded to sing (ll. 5–6), are propagandists
but poets first.

Windsor-Forest burgeons with metamorphoses, Lodona's the
most prominent, the least fanciful being those performed by
Pope's Horatian man as the description continues:

> He gathers Health from Herbs the Forest yields,
> And of their fragrant Physick spoils the Fields:
> With Chymic Art exalts the Min'ral Pow'rs,
> And draws the Aromatick Souls of Flow'rs.   (ll. 241–44)

The passage proceeds to further exaltation of his activities, none
of them in any sense aggressive (unless exceptional importance is

---

[2] This despite G. Wilson Knight's "So the courtier ranks above the poet, whose
'chymic art,' reading magic lore from nature and history and associated with god-
like excursions beyond earth and mortality, is a brilliantly characterized second"
in *Laureate of Peace* (New York, 1955), p. 21. Reuben A. Brower "distrusts Pope's
'Happy *next* him'" in context *(Alexander Pope: The Poetry of Allusion* [Oxford, 1959],
p. 58). Thomas R. Edwards, Jr. remarks that "Pope probably meant to give the
country poet second place, but the courtier's joys are summarily dropped while
rural retirement gets 22 lines of praise" (*This Dark Estate: A Reading of Pope* [Berke-
ley, 1963], p. 10). The couplet on the courtier (ll. 235–36) was an afterthought;
in the 1712 manuscript Pope begins the verse paragraph with "Happy the Man
who to the Shades retires" (Robert M. Schmitz, *Pope's Windsor Forest 1712: A Study
of the Washington University Holograph*, Washington University Studies, N.S., Language and Literature, No. 21 [St. Louis, 1952], p. 35). A comparable trope appears
in Pope's poetry many years later, in *An Epistle to Dr. Arbuthnot*, ll. 143–44: "Happy
my Studies, when by these [his famous friends] approv'd!/ Happier their Author,
when by these belov'd!"

attributed to the word "spoils"). For example, there is no discord whatsoever, no contrariety, in the combination of gathering and yielding; there is only active cooperation. Through several more lines the poem quietly traces this vein.

The activities of the Horatian man do not, conspicuously, include hunting, and in this respect he differs considerably from his queen and countrymen. Athrong with blood-sportsmen of all stations, the poem reviews those Norman Williams who preyed on men, then, throughout what amounts to Pope's *Seasons* (ll. 93–164), describes eighteenth-century swains who take to field and stream as eagerly as British infantry go to war, and seemingly more destructively: the prominent simile of neatly capturing "some thoughtless Town" immediately precedes those coruscant lines on the marvelous, bleeding pheasant. What Diana was to Arcadia, England's Queen and Huntress Anna is to Windsor; but Anna is also "Empress of the Main" (l. 164), and in that capacity recalls the cautionary example of errant Lodona: hunting is dangerous, an analogue of war as the poet often shows. One can, Lodona's story warns, go beyond the bounds of safety—as Anne must know, having urged an end to England's foreign war; as Anne must remember. Although conditions at home are better than they were when Norman kings proscribed hunting (in a sense, a decent law) but proved themselves indifferent to homicide, life still has perils. Although the queen, who conserves the forest beasts and her nation, represents a vast improvement over former royalty, her position remains precarious, in foreign affairs at least, and her albeit provident behavior lacks the refinement of the Horatian man's.

He is not, however, an outright pacifist. Addressing the Thames, he rejoices to think that "future Navies," not just merchant ships, are growing on the banks (l. 222). Addressing Granville, he lauds England's heroes. But he concentrates on

war's sorrows as he comes to the end of his address and to another panegyrical couplet more questionable than those written
before:

> What Tears has *Albion* shed,
> Heav'ns! What new Wounds, and how her old have bled?
> She saw her Sons with purple Deaths expire,
> Her sacred Domes involv'd in rolling Fire,
> A dreadful Series of Intestine Wars,
> Inglorious Triumphs, and dishonest Scars.
> At length great *ANNA* said—Let Discord cease!
> She said, the World obey'd, and all was *Peace!*   (ll. 321–28)

Here is all the lofty majesty, and all the unreality, of the wishful
conclusion to *Absalom and Achitophel,* wherein Dryden prophesied
a swift divine fiat to resolve the Exclusion Crisis. Britain had not
secured peace at home and abroad by declaring it; she had won
it by effecting or threatening destruction on the battlefield, on
the seas, in Parliament, and at Utrecht. Moreover, "Let Discord
cease" seems hardly the appropriate proclamation, for discord,
in what passes for the poem's dominant metaphor, lives in the
nature of the universe, ineradicable. The peacemaker can hope
for nothing better than to yoke its elements with an oxymoron.
Peace has been compelled, imposed by the ravages of a long war
and by the prospect of further woe if warfare persists. In an earlier version of *Windsor-Forest,* as the Twickenham editors note,
Anne's words had been "Let there be Peace," Pope's modification
suggesting that the accuracy of her proclamation resides in its
negativeness, peace being more than the absence of war. But what
business does the private man have to philosophize thus soberly
on so joyous and promising, if imperfect, an occasion as that
offered by the Treaty? And what chance does he have of being
heeded by the mighty? None.

Hence the introduction of a more exalted personage, Father Thames, who enters to rejoice in what has been achieved as he anticipates increasing prosperity now that England has peace (though not all nations do). He sees farther still; his prophecy rolls along through ages, all but imperceptibly. Through line 384 he speaks of England as Queen Anne shall continue to rule her, as man's aggression shall continue to be satisfied in hunting. Yet after that line he seems to gather breath and launch himself toward a point far in the future. Commerce will satisfy aggression, we are told at first in sanguinary lines that seem to represent an advance upon hunting, a readjustment of the object to a station somewhat lower on the Great Chain: "For me the Balm shall bleed, and Amber flow,/ The Coral redden, and the Ruby glow" (ll. 393–94); remember the Horatian man and the spoils of the fields. Then the omega point becomes visible; the terrestrial paradise—more Edenic, even, than the Forest preserve sung at the outset of the poem—rises before us:

> The Time shall come, when free as Seas or Wind
> Unbounded Thames shall flow for all Mankind,
> Whole Nations enter with each swelling Tyde,
> And Seas but join the Regions they divide;
> Earth's distant Ends our Glory shall behold,
> And the new World launch forth to seek the Old.
> Then Ships of uncouth Form shall stem the Tyde,
> And Feather'd People crowd my wealthy Side,
> And naked Youths and painted Chiefs admire
> Our Speech, our Colour, and our strange Attire!
> Oh stretch thy Reign, fair *Peace!* from Shore to Shore,
> Till Conquest cease, and Slav'ry be no more. . . .   (ll. 397–408)

This is the reign not of Anne and, however acceptably terminated, conquest, but of Peace herself. This is a time when all dangerous division has evaporated, a period in which men come together from all over, for trade, indeed, but seemingly more so from curiosity, emulating the Horatian man as he explores nature.[3] The new world seeks the old as the forest yields him health.

Worth particular note is the phrase "Feather'd People," stock diction for *birds*, here revivified to suggest a time when the barbarian men England exploits as she does her pheasants shall be more than welcome on her shores, a time when the natural and the social, each signified in that phrase, shall be as one. There is no contrariety, only variety, in this vision.

> Till Conquest cease, and Slav'ry be no more:
> Till the freed *Indians* in their native Groves
> Reap their own Fruits, and woo their Sable Loves,
> *Peru* once more a Race of Kings behold,
> And other *Mexico's* be roof'd with Gold.
> Exil'd by Thee from Earth to deepest Hell,
> In Brazen Bonds shall barb'rous Discord dwell. . . .   (ll. 408–14)

Then shall discord give way to concord, remotely then: the Twickenham editors observe wryly that a treaty made with Spain at Utrecht, the Asiento, gave Britain a thirty-year monopoly on importation of slaves to the Spanish colonies; it scarcely needs noting that Pope's lines on the Indians, Incas and Aztecs, strike discordantly against what the eighteenth century thought permissible

---

[3] A passage in Werner Jaeger's *Paideia* may nicely illuminate this point. Describing the new state envisioned in Plato's *Laws,* Jaeger observes, "No citizen may travel abroad except heralds, ambassadors, and '*theoroi*': by which Plato does not mean the cities' representatives at festivals (the usual sense of the word), but men with the spirit of scientific research who will go abroad to *theorein*, to 'contemplate' the civilization and laws of other men and study conditions abroad at their leisure. Without knowledge of men good and bad, no state can become perfect or preserve its laws. The chief aim of such journeys abroad is that the *theoroi* should meet the few distinguished personalities or 'divine men' who exist in the mass of ordinary people, and whom it is worth meeting and talking to" *(Paideia,* tr. Gilbert Highet [New York, 1944], III, 259). Pope's Indians would therefore seek out Englishmen like the Horatian denizen of Windsor Forest.

expedients of trade. There shall then be positive peace, based not on commercial competition but, seemingly, on propriety, on mankind's having achieved self-possession, just as the native Americans shall have been yielded their rightful land and liberty. Discord shall have been expelled by a force superior to it, Peace herself, not Anna. The world shall have seen its finest metamorphosis.

I would conclude this chapter with an appreciative remark about Pope's four-hundredth line, "And Seas but join the Regions they divide," which continues to strike me as a small coup of the poetic imagination—imagination transcending the imaginable; I would end on this point if other matters did not require mention, matters relating to Virgil, whose poems underlie *Windsor-Forest* from start to finish. Earl R. Wasserman discovered that the speech of Father Thames "echoes the prophecy of an Augustan Golden Age in the sixth book of the *Aeneid*"; the Twickenham editors appropriately cite Virgil's *Georgics* and *Pollio*, the fourth *Eclogue*, in connection with the end of Father Thames's speech.[4] But both Wasserman and the editors ignore a portion of the *Eclogue* which provides a model for the progressive series of eras that Father Thames foretells, the series culminating in renewal of the Golden Age. Virgil's messianic youth shall bind in peace the discordant "jarring nations" (the translation is Dryden's, l. 20), but not immediately. Although he shall early see the soil minister to him, providing harvests without human labor,

> Yet of old fraud some footsteps shall remain:
> The merchant still shall plow the deep for gain. . . .
> Another Helen other wars create
> And great Achilles urge the Trojan fate.

[4] Wasserman, p. 166; E. Audra and Aubrey Williams, eds., Introduction to *Windsor-Forest*, in *Pastoral Poetry and An Essay on Criticism*, Vol. I of the Twickenham Edition (London, 1961), pp. 142–44.

> But when to ripen'd manhood he shall grow,
> The greedy sailer shall the seas forego;
> No keel shall cut the waves for foreign ware,
> For every soil shall every product bear.   (ll. 37–38, 43–48)

Both warfare *and* commerce shall have been superseded. The association of commerce with warfare points to Pope's poem and especially to the end of it, when general self-possession, propriety, makes obsolete the urge to acquire property. A condition in which every land can produce everything is symbolic of *concordia discors* —but of it only as variety in unity, no longer as opposing elements yoked. The condition foretold is really a *concordia*, period.

When Father Thames's speech is finished, Pope has an opportunity to comment, but deferentially he will not. That, the final lines tell, is matter for the courtier-poet Granville, who as Her Majesty's Secretary at War is in a position to inform the queen and the nations about true peace, to elaborate and implement the vision of godly Thames. Already knowing such peace, Pope will modestly continue to possess his soul in his own quarter of the forest,

> Where Peace descending bids her Olives spring,
> And scatters Blessings from her Dove-like Wing.
> Ev'n I more sweetly pass my careless Days,
> Pleased in the silent Shade with empty Praise;
> Enough for me, that to the listning Swains
> First in these Fields I sung the Sylvan Strains.   (ll. 429–34)

There the bird of peace flies unthreatened, at least by the happier man. The words "more sweetly" make sure we recognize who that is, the man who rates self-approval over praise, who knows peace is more than a stand-off, and who speaks his mind, to an audience disposed to listen. Playing dumb, recurring in the last line to the simple first line of the *Pastorals*, Pope's speaker points the way to a perfect world, from his sanctuary.

3. The Rape of the Lock: Sublunary Belinda

"Oh say what stranger Cause, yet unexplor'd/ Cou'd make a gentle *Belle* reject a *Lord?*" A pertinent question, this from the beginning of Pope's droll epyllion, and not the only question a reader might ask about the fictional process, the fable, of the poem. What happens is evident enough: Belinda loses her heart, her lock, and her temper, in that order—but how, why? How, especially, does she happen to fall in love when so thoroughly protected from just that eventuality by the busy sylphs? An answer to this and other productive questions entails some preliminary description of Belinda's world and cosmos, and of her narrator's peculiar point of view.

The Rape of the Lock is full of a number of things, in its resplendent artifice recalling the enameled Christmas world of *Sir Gawain and the Green Knight*. Yet the tinsel things surrounding, including, Belinda prove dangerous, threatening to overcome and stifle nature. Fittingly, therefore, the right relation of mankind to things—a topic ubiquitous in Pope's poems—matters greatly in the moral center of the poem, Clarissa's speech (v.9–34), still more in the speech from the *Iliad* upon which Pope modeled it. There, in Book XII, Sarpedon tells Glaucus that aristocrats like themselves merit the luxuries they enjoy because, when a

higher good demands it, they have the self-control to forgo those
luxuries, a strength rooted in awareness of the transience of
enjoyments. Likewise, Clarissa argues that because there is no
permanence in material, sensible things, a woman must exert
her own power rather than submit to theirs. Affection dependent
on the senses turns out to be insufficient: "Charms strike the
Sight, but Merit wins the Soul"—Nestorean words for a young
lady too headstrong or weak-witted to heed them.

Belinda fails to imitate responsive Glaucus. Her narrator,
though fully conversant with the epic's main roads, departs
somewhat from them: despite his abundant allusions to Homer,
Virgil, and Milton, the cosmos of *The Rape of the Lock* has less in
common with that of the *Iliad, Odyssey, Aeneid,* or *Paradise Lost*
than with that of Chaucer's *Knight's Tale.* What hierarchy controls
Pope's universe? In Chaucer, the Olympian gods are redefined
by the end of the poem, becoming astrological: Mars turns out
to be a planet rather than the Greek divinity of Homer. The
planets execute man's fate, but do not determine it; determina-
tion is the inscrutable business of the remote, unseen "Firste
Moevere." Whether man has freedom remains an open question—
whether Arcite's praying for victory instead of for Emily should
be classified as an error or simply as just another link in the
celestially predetermined chain of events. Certainly, however,
the emphasis of the *Tale* is upon acceptance of a not perfectly
intelligible universe rather than upon the value of circumspection
in decision-making. Says Theseus: "Thanne is it wysdom, as it
thinketh me,/ To maken vertu of necessitee . . ." (ll. 3041–42).

The narrative point of view assumed by Homer, Virgil, and
Milton approaches omniscience; Chaucer's does not. The former
poets, at home with immortals as well as with us, in general
speak as fully describing celestial events as they do when dealing
with the earthly. But Chaucer, and Pope, seem to see less. Chaucer's stellar gods are the *proximate* divinities; we hear them speak,

but what the Prime Mover is thinking we never learn. Pope's sylphs, the light militia of the *lower* sky (1.42), are but one class of a gradated divine corporation, as Ariel explains to the sylphs he commands:

> Ye know the Spheres and various Tasks assign'd,
> By Laws Eternal, to th' Aerial Kind.
> Some in the Fields of purest AEther play,
> And bask and whiten in the Blaze of Day.
> Some guide the Course of wandering Orbs on high,
> Or roll the Planets thro' the boundless Sky.
> Some less refin'd, beneath the Moon's pale Light
> Pursue the Stars that shoot athwart the Night,
> Or suck the Mists in grosser Air below,
> Or dip their Pinions in the painted Bow,
> Or brew fierce Tempests on the wintry Main,
> Or o'er the Glebe distill the kindly Rain.
> Others on Earth o'er human Race preside,
> Watch all their Ways, and all their Actions guide:
> Of these the Chief the Care of Nations own,
> And guard with Arms Divine the *British Throne*.
>   Our humbler Province is to tend the Fair,
> Not a less pleasing, tho' less glorious Care.   (II.75–92)

As the poem so efficiently reveals, the sylphs' power has limits. What power they possess depends upon women's constancy, the rejection of lovers in favor of sylphs (1.67–68). The sylphs' resources for maintaining such constancy, limited also, Ariel describes later in the same expository speech:

> Oft when the World imagine Women stray,
> The *Sylphs* thro' mystick Mazes guide their Way,
> Thro' all the giddy Circle they pursue,
> And old Impertinence expel by new.
> What tender Maid but must a Victim fall
> To one Man's Treat, but for another's Ball?
> When *Florio* speaks, what Virgin could Withstand,
> If gentle *Damon* did not squeeze her Hand?
> With varying Vanities, from ev'ry Part,

They shift the moving Toyshop of their Heart;
Where Wigs with Wigs, with Sword-knots Sword-knots strive,
Beaus banish Beaus, and Coaches Coaches drive.
This erring Mortals Levity may call,
Oh blind to Truth! the *Sylphs* contrive it all.   (I.91–104)

By *somehow* parading vanities before a girl, the sylphs keep her
in motion, unattached to any single suitor, for like an infant the
coquette has not learned to distinguish and separate any single
element from the continuum of experience. The sylphs keep
her hovering in air, their element, preoccupied with the surfaces
of a processive series of things—*things*. On the surface, a lapdog
and a husband or a snuffbox and a beau may seem very much
alike, objects; a bible as such belongs with puffs and patches.
That some objects are, in addition, human—objects of love,
not mere *objets d'art*—will not occur to the girl on the go,
and does not seem evident to Ariel either, to judge by his in-
discriminate list of potential "disasters" (II.105–10). Those
accounted sane in such a world see people as objects; the insane,
objects as people: living teapots and the like (IV.49–54).

The sylphs guard women, men are on their own. And whereas
the coquette moves among many admirers, shining "on all alike"
(II.14), a man chooses a single belle; that is, he concentrates on
one at a time. But because all the coquette's charm radiates from
her surface, the lover perceives only what, in "A Digression
on Madness" of *A Tale of a Tub*, Swift calls the "*Superficies* of
Things"; it is things which fascinate the Baron, fetishes: "three
Garters, half a Pair of Gloves;/ And all the Trophies of his
former Loves" (II.39–40; also II.23–28).[1] The elaborate lock

[1] Geoffrey Tillotson half-humorously noted the Baron's possible "hair fetich-
ism," *The Rape of the Lock and Other Poems*, Vol. II of the Twickenham Edition
(3d ed., London, 1962), p. 91*n*. Jeffrey Meyers explores the psychoanalytical
implications in "The Personality of Belinda's Baron: Pope's 'The Rape of the
Lock,'" *American Imago*, XXVI (1969), 71–77. "The Case of Miss Arabella Fermor,"
as delightfully described by Cleanth Brooks in chapter 5 of *The Well Wrought
Urn* (New York, 1947), should not go unmentioned.

seems as attractive as Belinda, indeed preferable, to the experienced Baron; the etymological kinship of *artifact* and *fetish*
is worth keeping in mind. This state of affairs, this sterile economy, is just what the sylphs require and promote in their province
of the universe, and thus do they manipulate belles, indirectly
beaus, to control polite society. Perverse or at least self-centered,
the sylphs distort human life by making people attend only to
material things; worse, things seen not as they are but either
superficially or figuratively.

But in the course of Canto III the sylphic economy suddenly
collapses. Although Belinda enters the card game with a gregar-
iousness Ariel would approve, lining up her succession of intended victims—

> *Belinda* now, whom Thirst of Fame invites,
> Burns to encounter two adventrous Knights,
> At *Ombre* singly to decide their Doom;
> And swells her Breast with Conquests yet to come. (III.25–28)

—yet by line 144 she has somehow broken Ariel's spell, has fallen
in love or at least feels passion for, or attraction toward, one
man. The sylph's control lapses as he looks within her and discovers "An Earthly Lover lurking at her Heart." How did the
lover, presumably the Baron, get there? Had his near-victory at
cards forced her to concentrate upon him really "singly," to the
exclusion of all other men? In the course of the game Belinda
did, for the first time in the poem, show discomposure, trembling
"in the Jaws of Ruin, and *Codille*" when the Knave of Diamonds
won the Queen of Hearts (III.87–92).

Or does the explanation lurk in physiology? Cards put aside,
the players had turned to coffee:

> *Coffee,* (which makes the Politician wise,
> And see thro' all things with his half-shut Eyes)
> Sent up in Vapours to the *Baron's* Brain
> New Stratagems, the radiant Lock to gain. (III. 117–20)

Here again, perhaps, Swift on his sooty Pinions flitts, the innovative effects of vapors from below being another salient topic of "A Digression on Madness." Belinda's crisis coincides with her taking of coffee, "As o'er the fragrant Steams she bends her Head" (III.134). It is while Ariel watches "th' Ideas rising in her Mind" (III.142) that he perceives the lover at her heart, the "Earthly" lover.

What has happened, I would suggest, is that Belinda has become materialistic in a new way; that Pope, like Lucretius, has emphatically asserted the connection between things and thoughts; that the sylph's vapid Platonism has been penetrated by the obtrusion of hard, particular philosophical materialism; that the power deep in things, shattering surfaces, has burst upward to bring hovering Belinda down with a bump. Actuality, to the extent that matter constitutes it, has broken in. Ariel himself has possibly been taken in by his own contrivances, neglectful of what he would have had Belinda ignore, that there is more to things than meets the eye.

The Baron, after all, is a hog from Epicurus' herd, a man one might encounter in Lucretius had the Roman written on the nature of the *haut monde*. His vaunt becomes a paean to the perdurability, even the ontological supremacy, of tangible substance:

> What Time wou'd spare, from Steel receives its date,
> And Monuments, like Men, submit to Fate!
> Steel cou'd the Labour of the Gods destroy. . . .   (III. 171–73)

Fate is identical with matter, to him. Now he has the sought, immortal thing, the lock, in his hand. Now, the sylphs dispersed, Belinda falls prey to another sort of daemon, the gnome Umbriel, for the thought of an earthly lover has disposed her to receive an earthly spirit, who travels in a vapor like coffee's (IV.18). The gnome's first destination, though, is a dismal infernal palace hung round with a "constant *Vapour*" (IV.39), the abode of the

"Parent of Vapors" (IV. 59), Spleen—a goddess on a level of divine
being different from those to which readers have thus far been
introduced. Spleen outranks Umbriel. (Who, one might ask par-
enthetically, is Ariel's chief?) Submissive Umbriel procures bag
and vial, vents them on Belinda, and the result bodes war. No
longer manipulated by means of superficial things, she is now
the slave of her spleen, her insides, her deep corporeality, recognized by her for the first time. Forgotten, of course, is Ariel's
advice, "Nor bound thy narrow Views to Things below" (I.36).

Here Clarissa plays Cassandra, in her speech—added in 1717
"to open more clearly the MORAL of the Poem," according to
Pope's note (an unheeded prophetess may be added anytime)—in
her speech providing a direct criticism of the two kinds of en-
slavement Belinda has known, the sylphs' insubstantial vanity
and the gnomes' gross humor. The remedy: another sort of
humor. "Good Humour can prevail,/When Airs, and Flights,"
manifestations of sylphic superficiality, "and Screams, and Scold-
ing," gnomic ventings, "fail" (v.31–32). Optimistically reposing
all one's trust in beauty, pessimistically concentrating upon what
"shall fade," both attitudes are fallacious. Instead a girl should
assert her autonomy, make up her mind and will, use her "Pow'r,"
not abandon herself to the force of vanity and vapors, "keep good
Humor still whate'er we lose" (v.27, 29–30). These are sensible
words, but in vain; as the Baron's accomplice in the snipping of
the lock, Clarissa does speak at a disadvantage. The ladies arm for
war, spleen possessing them, the gnome presiding over the conflict (v. 53–54). Near the end of the battle comes Belinda's *aristeia*,
in which her new allies the gnomes fully discharge their Lucretian responsibilities:

> A Charge of *Snuff* the wily Virgin threw;
> The Gnomes direct, to ev'ry Atome just,
> The pungent Grains of titillating Dust.   (v. 82–84)

But Lucretius will not be permitted the last word.[2] Inexplicably, according to Belinda or the Baron's way of reasoning, the lock is gone, to become a comet or a shooting star: "A sudden Star, it shot thro' liquid Air . . ." (v.127)—at which Belinda, the poet tells her, ought to be pleased like the sylphs (v.131–32); but the routed sylphs may be glad their supplanters, the gnomes, have also been frustrated. "Then cease, bright Nymph! to mourn thy ravish'd Hair/Which adds new Glory to the shining Sphere!" (v.141–42). How may Lucretius' theory explain that? It cannot, and Pope will not try to explain, to Belinda. There are more things in heaven than are dreamt of in her philosophy.[3] Instead he pays her a courtly compliment, fair-sexing her. The factitious beau monde, the mistaken "blest Lover," and inane Partridge will note the new star; Belinda will have fame; yet so did tragic, short-sighted Achilles, with whom she has several times been identified, and Chaucer's Arcite. People will remember her, intelligent people to regret that she could not bring herself to heed Clarissa's advice. The narrator, mentioning the likes of Partridge with honor, speaks with tongue in cheek, but he has been doing so since the beginning of the poem. His pregnant reticence has been evident ever since he permitted Ariel's definition of "Honour" to pass unchallenged (I.78).

Who is Ariel's rightful chief? As may be recalled, Belinda does have a tutelary star that early in the poem hinted at the dread event impending, an event known then to "Heav'n" (I.lll), not to Belinda or to Ariel. And of the pluralistic "Aerial Kind," Pope had written (Ariel had admitted),

[2] L. C. Martin describes Pope's incidental debts to the Roman poet in "Lucretius and *The Rape of the Lock*," *Review of English Studies,* xx (1944), 299–303.

[3] James L. Jackson says the conflict "of the epic has been resolved . . . by the introduction of a force outside the action," in "Pope's *The Rape of the Lock* Considered as a Five-Act Epic," *PMLA,* lxv (1950), 1286. But it only seems as if this is the case, because the focus of the narrative induces in readers a myopia like Belinda's.

> Some guide the Course of wandring Orbs on high,
> Or roll the Planets thro' the boundless Sky.
> Some less refin'd, beneath the Moon's pale Light
> Pursue the Stars that shoot athwart the Night. . . .   (II.79–82)

Ariel, as he goes on to confess, is of the latter order. Umbriel's address to Spleen parodies Nisus' prayer to the moon in the *Aeneid*. "Dull sublunary" Belinda, "Whose soul is sense" in Donne's words from *A Valediction: Forbidding Mourning*, has been fitly commemorated in all her inadequate glory. Her lock in its apotheosis has become perhaps no more than a shooting star—a star, needless to say, of inferior magnitude, a meteor beneath the lunar sphere—as determined by fate, the stars, Heaven, all of them outside Ariel's province and beyond the range of Belinda's pseudo-solar eye.

I have dealt harshly with, even flayed, Belinda. So, I think, does Pope, but his severity is less evident than I have tried to make it, because he is clearly so appreciative of her beauty. "Charms strike the Sight." A poem, a fiction, a fable, however, has various significances if it is fine, sustaining them all, as Pope recognized in praising the *Iliad* for its lamination of the probable, the marvelous, and the allegorical. Of the *allegorical* fable he wrote: "If we reflect upon those innumerable Knowledges, those Secrets of Nature and Physical Philosophy which *Homer* is generally suppos'd to have wrapt up in his *Allegories*, what a new and ample Scene of Wonder may this Consideration afford us? How fertile will that Imagination appear, which was able to cloath all the Properties of Elements, the Qualifications of the Mind, the Virtues and Vices, in Forms and Persons; and to introduce them into Actions agreeable to the Nature of the Things they shadow'd?"[4] Yet, as he pointed out in his note prefatory to *The Temple of Fame*, "In Epick Poetry, 'tis true, too nice and exact

---

[4] "Preface," *The Iliad of Homer*, ed. Maynard Mack, Vol. VII of the Twickenham Edition (London, 1967), p. 6.

a Pursuit of the Allegory is justly esteem'd a Fault; and *Chaucer* had the discernment to avoid it in his *Knight's Tale*." Sparkling so from facets within facets, *The Rape of the Lock* may be enjoyed even when incompletely understood; indeed a reader has trouble tracing one line of meaning through it without being captivated at some point by another. Hence perhaps the difficulty presented by questions so simple as those I have tried to answer. Instead of merely digressing into the region of allegory, Pope there fulfills his fable, beautifully integrating both so thoroughly that one cannot be understood without recourse to the other. From an ultimate vantage point far removed above Belinda's, the narrator has made a world that moves, as he wishes it to, by itself, beneath him.

4. *Eloisa to Abelard*: *Une Lettre Philosophique*

"Their fate does not leave the mind in hopeless dejection; for they both found quiet and consolation in retirement and piety."[1] Thus Samuel Johnson on *Eloisa to Abelard*, or, perhaps more precisely, on the biographies of the lovers, for it is difficult to see how Eloisa's lament may be read as an advertisement for the consolations of retirement and piety.[2] Another early critic, Bishop Warburton's friend Owen Ruffhead, feared "it has done no service to the cause of virtue."[3] Eloisa's mental state from

---

[1] Samuel Johnson, "Pope," *Lives of the English Poets*, ed. George Birkbeck Hill (Oxford, 1905), III, 235.

[2] Difficult for me. Brendan O Hehir finds that, after Eloisa has discovered "the vanity of worldly commitments" in ll. 311–36, "No obstacles remain to the consummation of her marriage to Christ, and that consummation has also, paradoxically, a place for Abelard" ("Virtue and Passion: The Dialectic of *Eloisa to Abelard*," reprinted with corrections from *Texas Studies in Literature and Language*, II [1960], 219–32, in Maynard Mack, ed., *Essential Articles for the Study of Alexander Pope*, rev., enl. ed. [Hamden, Conn., 1968], p. 346). Abelard's place is to bring Eloisa the last rites, "The hallow'd taper trembling in thy hand" (l. 326). The ambivalence of such imagery at the supposed point of resolution makes O Hehir's interpretation itself seem paradoxical, if not simply mistaken. Henry Pettit's less sanguine essay in the same collection ("Pope's *Eloisa to Abelard*: An Interpretation," pp. 320–32), defending Eloisa for heroically resisting an extreme dualism, is more faithful to the poem.

[3] *The Life of Alexander Pope* (London, 1769), p. 171.

first to last is one of ineradicable anguish; had Johnson probed the poem he would have found it as disconcerting in some ways as Pope's *Elegy to the Memory of an Unfortunate Lady*, with its "illaudable singularity of treating suicide with respect."[4]

Eloisa's dilemma may be put succinctly: how can this nun accept Christ as her lover when she can envision a lover only in the person of Abelard? His castration is really inconsequential. Were he whole the problem would remain, transcendentally, to afflict Eloisa whether on earth or in the afterlife. Moreover, it is a problem generic to Christianity, present in the ethical core of Matthew's gospel, 22:35–40: "Then one of them, which was a lawyer, asked him a question, . . . which is the great commandment in the law? Jesus said unto him, Thou shalt love the Lord thy God with all thy heart, and with all thy soul, and with all thy mind. This is the first and great commandment. And the second is like unto it, Thou shalt love thy neighbor as thyself. On these two commandments hang all the law and the prophets." Without attempting thorough interpretation, I may distinguish a sense in which the second commandment is not like but potentially antithetical to the first, the sense in which the whole passage, while subsuming self-interest in love of God, recognizes the potency of self-interest, making it the measure of love of neighbor. The second commandment does not proceed from the first, as it would, for example, if it read "Thou shalt love thy neighbor as a creature of God like thyself." Rather, it begins in an observation, that men love themselves, which would appeal to philosophers like Locke or Montesquieu, or to the Pope who wrote, in *An Essay on Man*, that self-love and social love are the same (III.318, IV.396). The first commandment is patently revelatory in its absoluteness and and exclusiveness; the second has an empirical base, like Eloisa's reasoning. In case of conflict,

[4] Johnson, III, 226.

St. Paul had said (I Cor. 5:7; as had Christ: Matt. 5:27–30), pluck away the offending member; fate or Providence had in fact accomplished such for Abelard. But Paul had had that extraordinary experience on the road to Damascus, an advantage Eloisa, to her sorrow, has not received.

Her thoughts may be considered the materials of a case history describing the psychosis of a woman who cannot distinguish religious from erotic feeling, and indeed the poem is dazzling in this respect. Eloisa becomes a classic example of hysteria, a carnal St. Theresa whirled in a vortex of rampant subjectivity.[5] But it also can be argued, as I shall maintain here, that despite her apparent levitations Eloisa keeps her feet very much on the ground—not, however, sacred ground. One interpretation of the poem may regard her as a saint, if not of religion, of love. The present interpretation will praise her for her tenacity in attempting to think for herself, and there is some historical justification for my view.

It may be recalled that Pope's primary source was the translation of the letters (1713) made by John Hughes, Hughes's text being a fanciful French version with a preface based upon the lovers' history as told by none other than Pierre Bayle;[6] told, it may be added, with Bayle's customary subversiveness and fervor. To Bayle, Héloïse seemed in some ways a model of emancipation from overbearing authority, as appears most pointedly in the article he devoted to her in his famous *Dictionnaire historique et critique.* There and in the preface to the edition Hughes trans-

[5] Patricia Meyer Spacks compares Eloisa with a psychotic patient, arriving at quite negative opinions about the poem's merit, in *An Argument of Images: The Poetry of Alexander Pope* (Cambridge, Mass., 1971), pp. 237–40.

[6] Robert P. Kalmey, "Pope's *Eloisa to Abelard* and 'Those Celebrated Letters,'" *PQ* xlvii (1968), 168–69. Kalmey thinks the poem retains the essence of the Latin letters, "the Christian view of man humbled by his own weakness before a just but merciful God" (p. 169), but nowhere in the poem does Eloisa, the only speaker, outrightly acknowledge God's justice, much less His mercy.

lated—though not without qualification: Bayle does regard her
passion as an infirmity or *cette folie*—she is a heroine who boldly
preferred love to marriage, from motives Bayle defends with
quite unequivocal earnestness and sympathy.[7] The same point
has prominence in Pope's poem (ll. 73 ff.), his only large poem
without a single line written in his own voice, dramatic throughout. Considering the freedom this mode made available to the
poet, and the significance of Eloisa's example to Bayle, a man
among the foremost in the *avant-garde* of the Enlightenment,
it may not seem far-fetched for me to read the poem in a manner
less orthodox than usual.

Pope's Eloisa concentrates upon three periods in her life,
first the idyll she lived with Abelard before they were separated,
in a golden world, a state of nature integrated by their love:

> Oh happy state! when souls each other draw,
> When love is liberty, and nature, law:
> All then is full, possessing, and possest,
> No craving Void left aking in the breast:

[7] Pierre Bayle, *Dictionnaire historique et critique*, vii (Paris, 1820), 557–59, 564–65,
569–70. John Hughes, tr., *Letters of Abelard and Eloisa. With a particular Account
of their Lives, Amours, and Misfortunes* (London, 1788), pp. 19–23. In his recent
cultural history of the Enlightenment, Peter Gay describes Abelard's philosophy
as its liberalism anticipated that of the *philosophes*. But though the author of an
ethics entitled *Know Thyself*, Abelard nevertheless told Eloisa that he did not want
to be a philosopher if being one meant resisting Christ and St. Paul (*The Enlightenment: A Modern Interpretation*, I [New York, 1966], 232), a consideration germane
to the present essay, as are James E. Wellington's remarks about the ambiguity
of the poem's ending (*Eloise to Abelard with the Letters of Heloise to Abelard in the
Version by John Hughes(1713)*, University of Miami Critical Studies, No. 5 [Coral
Gables, 1965], pp. 59–60), and Barrett John Mandel's argument that Eloisa's
monologue terminates in "emotional frustration" ("Pope's 'Eloisa to Abelard,'"
Texas Studies in Literature and Language, ix [1967], 57–68). Pope knew and relished
Bayle's dictionary, in a letter of 1731 appreciatively comparing old Jacob Tonson
to it, "so full of Matter, Secret History, & Wit & Spirit" (*Correspondence*, ed. George
Sherburn [5 vols.; Oxford, 1956], iii, 176).

> Ev'n thought meets thought ere from the lips it part,
> And each warm wish springs mutual from the heart.
> This sure is bliss (if bliss on earth there be)
> And once the lot of *Abelard* and me.   (ll. 91–98)

The second period, the present, is a time vexed by insatiable longing. The third, the time of her death, when she shall finally be able to die to the world, looms also as a time of struggle since she is describing it during the present. *In extremis*, as she imagines herself, she fantasizes in a manner that recalls the lovers' former bliss: "Suck my last breath, and catch my flying soul!" (l. 324). How like the happy state where souls each other draw; it would require lengthy analysis to demonstrate most of the correspondences in so nervously organic a poem.

Only by dying will she be able to renounce the world and Abelard. How thoroughly she depends upon him, craves him; how self-regarding is her affection. And Abelard's response?—she does not describe it, although she conjectures that his life is "a long, dead calm of fix'd repose" (l. 251). Preeminently, Eloisa wants Abelard to come for *her* good, not his, so much so that only when she imagines herself dead does she manifest a tincture of agape, and when she does, her own ardor remains the measure of sufficient love.

> Oh death all-eloquent! you only prove
> What dust we doat on, when 'tis man we love.
>   Then too, when fate shall this fair frame destroy,
> (That cause of all my guilt, and all my joy)
> In trance ecstatic may thy pangs be drown'd,
> Bright clouds descend, and Angels watch thee round,
> From opening skies may streaming glories shine,
> And Saints embrace thee with a love like mine.   (ll. 335–42)

What is the meaning of the opening couplet? that death reveals man's dusthood? that death merely makes manifest what was known all the time? that only death will reveal it, unimaginable now? that death despite all its eloquence cannot lessen the doating?— *all* these answers, diminishing love's power no more than death's.

For all practical purposes, Abelard seems as good as dead. The nuns, apart from Eloisa, lie stone-cold in their acceptance of the cloister's walls. And God, if not dead, is in hiding. Only Eloisa seems alive, unable to see man as mere dust, loving Abelard as she loves herself, her one substantial referent. To be sure, in her long passage of conscientious meditation (ll. 177–206) she wishes the case were otherwise. Her soul thrashes helplessly in its attempts to purge itself of worldly desire without the benefit of a Pauline intervention, "But let heavn seize it, all at once 'tis fir'd,/Not touch'd, but rapt; not waken'd, but inspired!" (ll. 201–2). Yet as I have said, nothing of the kind has ever happened to her. Her epiphany was in Abelard: handsome, intelligent, virtuous—except perhaps in that he taught her "'twas no sin to love" (l. 68). She cannot bring herself to believe it *was;* it was *natural.* The one way she can .envision turning to God is by subduing "nature" (l. 203). If the poem, to adopt what Pope says of the letters in his Argument, presents a "lively . . . picture of the struggles of grace and nature, virtue and passion," it would seem that nature and passion win out in a combination that may be denominated virtue: heartfelt adherence to nature as she understands it. "Know then thyself, presume not God to scan" might be Eloisa's motto. She knows she once knew bliss, knows she now feels woe, and cannot imagine bliss except in the shape wherein she once intensely possessed it. As Hume might have made her say if she were a speaker in the *Dialogues Concerning Natural Religion,* that such bliss has become physically and spiritually inaccessible does not prove that it is to be found in Heaven. Her base of affection is adamantine: she speaks erotically of religion but not religiously of love; she does not wish "an Angel whom I lov'd a Man" (l. 70). Loving Abelard as herself, even just the idea of Abelard, she finds she cannot love God as much as He demands without annihilating herself. That, she cannot do, perhaps cannot responsibly do.

Had Johnson scrutinized the poem he might have discerned in Eloisa a vile cosmic Whig. While several of her classical references — calling herself a "Vestal," for example — simply suggest that she had been deep in Ovid's *Heroides* when Abelard's letter came, other such references say more:

> Should at my feet the world's great master fall,
> Himself, his throne, his world, I'd scorn 'em all:
> Not *Caesar's* empress wou'd I deign to prove. . . .   (ll. 85–87)

Momentarily the comment seems rendered to God, not Caesar; then she proceeds, a female Cato, and to God's divine right as formulated at Rome opposes concepts comparable to those in Locke's *Second Treatise on Government:* "Oh happy state! . . ./ When love is liberty, and nature, law" (ll. 91–92); the same line, in the past tense, appears when Pope describes the "State of Nature" in *An Essay on Man* (iii.208). How wryly in this context may one recall Locke's favorite euphemism for revolution, the "appeal to Heaven." Eloisa's appeal is to men, and might be conveyed in lines from Pope's *Prologue to Mr. Addison's Tragedy of Cato,* written three years before the poem at hand: "Dare to have sense your selves; . . ./ Be justly warm'd with your own native rage" (ll. 43–44), *sapere aude.* How courageous is her response to the image of Abelard's immolation:

> A naked Lover bound and bleeding lies!
> Where, where was *Eloise?* her voice, her hand,
> Her ponyard, had oppos'd the dire command.
> Barbarian stay! that bloody stroke restrain;
> The crime was common, common be the pain.   (ll. 101–4)

In the just state or world, punishment is administered with equity.

But Eloisa's identity as *philosophe* may be pressed too far. Here, for qualification, is the great turning-point of the poem:

> Come, with one glance of those deluding eyes,
> Blot out each bright Idea of the skies.
> Take back that grace, those sorrows, and those tears,
> Take back my fruitless penitence and pray'rs,
> Snatch me, just mounting, from the blest abode,
> Assist the Fiends and tear me from my God!
>   No, fly me, fly me! far as Pole from Pole;
> Rise *Alps* between us! and whole oceans roll!   (ll. 283–90)

Here the crescendo of "Come's" addressed to Abelard, extending through her monologue, reaches a stop. Here she first says *no*. Why?—because she has terrified herself by drawing the logical religious conclusion about her love. Throughout the poem she has rebelled not against God but against the order of things, the order God allows to exist. Indirectly rebelling against God, she does not seem an atheist, as indeed she is not. But with these lines the final object of her rebellion becomes overt, nature against the supernatural, and casting about for allies she finds them—horrible to say—in the only place she can, Hell. Appalled, she reacts violently, in doing so resembling a regenerate Faustus. She cannot maintain her empirical, secular, felt values against the orthodoxy in which she has been bred. A republican in the temporal sphere, she remains a Christian vis-à-vis eternity. She does not love God, but she cannot help fearing him.

And yet: the end of the poem demonstrates the authenticity of her self-bred response, for in trying to conform to God's demands she reintroduces her own. In apparently endless torment she looks to the only remedy, death—death not as fulfillment, however, but as release. From line 297 through most of the remainder, she dwells on thoughts of dying and its aftermath. Earlier she had imagined death as anticipated by a "blameless Vestal" who, in some lines of celestial epithalamion, went to savor "eternal day" in the bridal chamber of her Spouse (ll. 217–22). For Eloisa such is impossible: preferring Abelard to God, she cannot yield herself to the divine Bridegroom, even when in His omnipotence He shall have taken her in death. Her vision of dying, though complete with "roseate bow'rs" and other paraphernalia conformable to the ordinary vestal's expectations, proves on the whole distinctly different, a place of "eternal rest" (ll. 302, 319), "eternal sleep" (l. 313), forgetfulness (l. 314)— in short, a Lethean release from selfhood. Horrified by Hell, unattracted to Heaven, she wants to be left alone, deprived of consciousness, buried. Thus she proves once more a kind of *philosophe*, digging her toes firmly into this earth, bracing herself, and, in effect, testing God: she predicts that, thinking of the lovers' fate, "Devotion's self shall steal a thought from heav'n,/ One human tear shall drop, and be forgiv'n" (ll. 357–58), if God is as good as He is said to be. The coda, sometimes thought extraneous, carries the theme further in its unfortunately contracted final line: "He best can paint 'em, who shall feel 'em most." Only someone with a grasp of experience as tenacious as Eloisa's will be able to sympathize with her fierce, inextirpable empiricism, which lines from the elegy for the Unfortunate Lady gloss perfectly:

> Is it, in heav'n, a crime to love too well?
> To bear too tender, or too firm a heart,
> To act a Lover's or a *Roman's* part?
> Is there no bright reversion in the sky
> For those who greatly think, or bravely die? (ll. 6–10)

The freedom Pope achieved by speaking in Eloisa's voice

throughout the poem has, not very paradoxically, brought him
down to earth as never before. The narrators of the pastorals
and *The Rape of the Lock*, and the speaker of *Windsor-Forest*, speak
as if they were simply observers of earthly life, beyond participa-
tion in it, above it. All make their homes in a better world, where
poetry is spoken. Not Eloisa, however. Robert Langbaum, in
his otherwise superb book *The Poetry of Experience*, contrasts the
inescapably subjective dramatic monologues of the nineteenth
and twentieth centuries with *Eloisa to Abelard*, contending "that
Eloisa understands everything, even her own self-deceptions
and submerged motives, that she understands herself as an
observer would understand her."[8] But she does not—nor, it
seems, does her author, who is himself explicitly drawn within
the constrictions of her world at the end of the poem. There
are no detached observers in the world of her poem, and she
and her author here speak of a better world only with nostalgia
and despair, this commonplace world being the only one available and its limitations insuperable. She cannot be other than
herself, cannot see things other than as she continues to see
them, and cannot consciously reconcile herself to them, without
pretending to be other than she is. Whatever Pope's personal
motives, he here departs sharply from the objective viewpoint
of most of his earlier work, never to return except temporarily
(and questionably) in the first version of *The Dunciad*. From
An Essay on Man to the end of his career, his voice is always that
of a participant in whatever basic actions he describes, although
his major philosophical poem, when seen in the context of his
entire canon, will like *Eloisa to Abelard* seem to mark a transitional
stage in the process.

[8] Robert Langbaum, *The Poetry of Experience: The Dramatic Monologue in Modern Literary Tradition* (Norton Library ed.; New York, 1963), p. 148.

5. *An Essay on Man*: To Reason Right Is to Submit

Although the word for Pope's philosophy as expressed in the *Essay on Man* may be *temperate* (in his preliminary account of the "Design" he hoped it was), it will not serve to describe his tone of voice in some prominent sections of the poem—a tone that provokes curiosity about the speaker's personality and circumstances, as well as about the identity of the persons he addresses and the assumptions upon which he founds communication. "Of Systems possible, if 'tis confest/ That Wisdom infinite must form the best . . ." (I.43–44); despite the fact that *confession* is practically ambiguous and can refer to anything from a free profession of belief to a reluctant admission of guilt, to the present-day reader, though not to him alone, the major, most beggarly question assumed by Pope, the big *donum*, has to do with the existence and nature of the God whose ways the poet sets out to vindicate. *As* a poet, employing the resources of his calling, Pope proved himself somewhat heedful of the potential confessor's difficulties, or so I shall maintain in examining the tone and action of the *Essay*. I begin with simpler matters and an unavoidably long quotation:

Awake my St. John! leave all meaner things
To low ambition, and the pride of Kings.
Let us (since Life can little more supply
Than just to look about us and to die)
Expatiate free o'er all this scene of Man;
A mighty maze! but not without a plan;
A Wild, where weeds and flow'rs promiscuous shoot,
Or Garden, tempting with forbidden fruit.
Together let us beat this ample field,
Try what the open, what the covert yield;
The latent tracts, the giddy heights explore
Of all who blindly creep, or sightless soar;
Eye Nature's walks, shoot Folly as it flies,
And catch the Manners living as they rise;
Laugh where we must, be candid where we can;
But vindicate the ways of God to Man.
    I. Say first, of God above, or Man below,
What can we reason, but from what we know?
Of Man what see we, but his station here,
From which to reason, or to which refer?
Thro' worlds unnumber'd tho' the God be known,
'Tis ours to trace him only in our own.
He, who thro' vast immensity can pierce,
See worlds on worlds compose one universe,
Observe how system into system runs,
What other planets circle other suns,
What vary'd being peoples ev'ry star,
May tell why Heav'n has made us as we are.
But of this frame the bearings, and the ties,
The strong connections, nice dependencies,
Gradations just, has thy pervading soul
Look'd thro'? or can a part contain the whole?
    Is the great chain, that draws all to agree,
And drawn supports, upheld by God, or thee?
    II. Presumptuous Man!   (I. 1–35)

The passage is puzzling: is that final accusation in any sense
addressed to Bolingbroke? Yes, since Bolingbroke comes under

the general heading Man, but how rapidly Pope has accelerated from tranquillity to contempt! Spoken to Bolingbroke, the first sixteen lines invite the nobleman to take part actively in a liberal, collaborative, occasionally amusing philosophical excursion, the first-person plurals suggesting dialogue. "Say first" the next line begins. From this point, however, the passage is directed increasingly toward the reader, who would seem to be the person mainly attacked at the end, and Bolingbroke goes unmentioned until Epistle iv. The reader too attentive to forget Bolingbroke's presence may regard him as a kind of prop, not unlike an attractive woman in an advertisement for something else.

And the *Essay* is not a dialogue, it is a speech, a passionate forensic plea.[1] Here and there one hears voices other than Pope's: Nature speaks in Epistle iii, Pride in Epistle i, an *adversarius* of sorts in Epistle iv. But except in the case of Nature, with whom I shall be concerned later, these appearances matter little, do not yield dramatization worth emphasis, amount to parodic impersonation by the speaker, for Pride's exchange with him (i. 132–48) is so full of accommodation that potentially separate characters merge, and the putative adversary, so late finding his tongue, may

---

[1] Martin Kallich aptly describes the poem's conversational quality as an "image," though he fails to recognize just how overbearing the speaker is (*Heav'n's First Law: Rhetoric and Order in Pope's Essay on Man* [DeKalb, Ill., 1967], p. 40). Maynard Mack, contrasting Pope's tone against the cool rationality of Dryden's *Religio Laici*, writes more perceptively in his rich introduction to the *Essay* (Vol. iii-i of the Twickenham Edition [London, 1950], pp. lxxix–lxxx). That Pope recognized a double standard in *An Essay on Man* permitting fast-and-loose play with his reader is clear in a letter to Caryll of September, 1732, where speaking of his current works, including the *Essay*, he says, "Let it suffice to tell you that they are directed to a good end, the advancement of moral and religious vertue, and the discouragement of vicious and corrupt hearts. As to the former, I treat it with the uttmost seriousness and respect; as to the latter, I think any means are fair and any method equal, whether preaching or laughing, whatever will do best" (*Correspondence,* ed. George Sherburn [5 vols.; Oxford, 1956], iii, 316).

also be described as a series of rhetorical questions. One of his five single-line comments still bears a narrative tail: "What differ more (you cry) than crown and cowl?" (iv. 199). No, if the *Essay* seems dramatic its drama must be located in the conflict to which the essayist responds, the tension which his tone implies. He *is* troubled, no longer the temperate, ingratiating exponent of the *Essay on Criticism,* not at all the descendant of that fond, patient, cordial Lucretius who told his noble friend Memmius about everything in *De Rerum Natura,* hardly the levelheaded, even-tempered successor to the Dryden of *Religio Laici,* to name some comparable works.

The unsignal "Say first" introduces a series of questions spaced by a passage (i. 21–28) declaring that human nature can be fathomed by an omniscient being. The opening questions have about them an aura of sweet logicality, have in fact the transparency of the self-evident. There is nothing surprising in their manner; honest Pope is beginning with fundamentals. But how different his tone at the end of the quotation! The declarative lines having introduced the example of an omniscient man, Pope abruptly asks the reader whether *he* is omniscient. Even more abruptly, Pope has assumed the reader thinks he is, the reader with his supposedly "pervading soul" (one learns later, at i.268, that only God has such). Finally, "Is the great chain, that draws all to agree,/ And drawn supports, upheld by God, or thee?" Presumptuous Pope! With monstrous incivility he has assumed that his silent reader (1) thinks himself the knower of all, or at least conducts himself as if he did; (2) thinks himself the equal of God, the sustainer of being. On what evidence does Pope base these assumptions? None within the poem, unless that hinted at by the depth of the speaker's feelings. "Fool!" he thunders repeatedly. "Go, wiser thou," "Go wond'rous creature," he presses the reader down with heavy sarcasm. As the poem unfolds its list of follies and evils the reader sees why Pope is so exercised, what wrongs the reader represents as one of the crass human herd.

Furthermore, in those initial thirty-five lines Pope has also defined or circumscribed the possibilities of knowledge. Either one knows what God knows or what the reader is presumed to know: everything, that is, or nothing. Or, if one will heed Pope, something: what Pope knows, and alluring Bolingbroke. Who is the "guide, philosopher, and friend"? He is a man who, at the onset of the Hanoverians, had suffered and survived, a cosmopolitan, an aristocrat, a free responsible spirit, the philosopher of Opposition to venality, a man now enjoying retirement with dignity, a man familiar with the vanities and contemptuous of them, apart—a man one might be proud to call one's associate. Together he and Pope stand as if above Dover Beach, where the reader may join them if he will, but he must not dally for the time is short, too short for nice philosophical qualifications, for hedging, for eclecticism of a fastidious kind. Hence the speaker's urgency, the broadness of his categories, the invariable yes-or-no of the choices offered. The speaker hastes on inexorably; the reader must run, ratifying essential principles as he goes, or fall by the wayside into unproductive scrupulosity. Seen from a Lucretian standpoint, what Pope has done is to divide the Memmius figure into two, the approved Bolingbroke and the candidate-reader, promising redintegration if the reader proves docile.[2] A look at the barren locale

[2] Something of a simplification regarding Lucretius, whose guide and philosopher is Epicurus and who can speak critically of Memmius, as at the end of Book III—but never speaks as sharply to him as Pope does to *his* reader. Interestingly, in the Morgan Library manuscript Epistle I begins, "Awake my Memmius, leave all meaner things . . ."; see *An Essay on Man: Reproductions of the Manuscripts in the Pierpont Morgan Library and the Houghton Library with the Printed Text of the Original Edition*, intro. Maynard Mack (Oxford, 1962).

of Pope's drawing, the frontispiece of the Twickenham Edition, with its crowded reminders of mutability—broken statues, columns, walls: death even in Arcady—will not encourage the reader to delay his commitment;[3] that is, his submission to the demands of the somewhat coercive, elitist speaker.

The reader may be saved, as the poem's passages of rapture imply; the vision is available. Indeed Pope juxtaposes carrot with whip, almost like a team of interrogators alternating lines of cordiality with lines of reprobation, consoling as well as threatening, sometimes befriending the reader, sometimes menacing him. If proliferation of identities were desirable one could argue that there are two Pope's speaking, the Pope who scolds, the Pope who embraces, for sometimes he admits the reader into a warm "we" or "our," though more frequently he chills him with "thou" or sharp imperatives. After fulmination like "All this dread ORDER break—for whom? for thee?/ Vile worm!—oh Madness, Pride, Impiety!" (1.257–58) what a pleasure it is to hear a simple, not inhospitable couplet like "Cease then, nor ORDER Imperfection name:/ Our proper bliss depends on what we blame" (1.281–82). Sometimes, too, the poet becomes so rapt in his topic that he forgets about his reader, lets him rest awhile. Neglect seems a blessing after abuse.

Pope proves most antagonistic in Epistle I, least in Epistle IV. In the first, besides the sections I have quoted, there is that ending "be the GOD of GOD!" (ll. 113–22), followed by an indulgent "In Pride, in reas'ning Pride, our error lies." For the most part, to the reader's relief, the poet speaks about not particular him but Man— with enough imperatives (Say, Hope, Wait, Lo! See . . .) and rhetorical questions to keep the reader constantly alert. Each of

[3] See Georgio Melchiori, "Pope in Arcady: The Theme of *Et in Arcadia Ego* in His Pastorals," *English Miscellany: A Symposium of History, Literature, and the Arts,* XIV (1963), 83–93.

the next two epistles has a sharply scornful cluster of lines very near the beginning: "Go, wond'rous creature! . . . / Then drop into thyself, and be a fool!" (ii.19–30); "Has God, thou fool! work'd solely for thy good . . . ?" (iii.27 ff.). Pope reminds the reader to be wary but generally concentrates on Man, with many scattered, incidental hints of encouragement: signs, for example, that tutor and pupil are of the same species after all: "Reason bids us for our own provide" (ii.96), "We, wretched subjects" (ii.149), "to mourn our Nature, not to mend" (ii.153). Epistles iii and iv each begin with comparable warmth: "Here then we rest" and "Oh happiness! our being's end and aim!" And the final epistle has only two harsh personal lines (173, 189), a series of acerb statements that are conditional (ll. 209–15), and another passage that is quite generalized:

> Oh sons of earth! attempt ye still to rise,
> By mountains pil'd on mountains, to the skies?
> Heav'n still with laughter the vain toil surveys,
> And buries madmen in the heaps they raise.   (ll. 73–76)

In the two-hundredth line the poet even calls the reader "friend," though not entirely unambiguously; at the same time, references to nearly forgotten Bolingbroke draw the nobleman closer (ll. 18, 240, 260). Indeed, near the end Pope seems to be preaching, finally, for his own and Bolingbroke's benefit, describing a man who is perfect, a model for each of them (ll. 330–52), and at last praising Bolingbroke as a better teacher than himself (ll. 373 ff.). It appears at this point that the whole *Essay* has been simply a menu for the feast of reason about to begin when Bolingbroke speaks. And the reader? He has perhaps been admitted into this party of virtue, for the last lines are all first-person-plural accord: "That Virtue only makes our Bliss below;/ And all our Knowledge is, ourselves to know." The host of exemplary personages in the fourth epistle,

vous autres, many of them cautionary exemplars, provides a suffi-
ciency of objects for raillery.

The part of the poem containing fewest accusations and
imperatives comes in the latter half of Epistle III, the lines surrounding Nature's theophany. The reader may relax for a while
as the poet turns away and the screen is illuminated with a docu-
mentary on the infancy and maturation of human society. This
prehistory seems especially revealing as the one section of the
poem that depends heavily upon experience of the past, imaginary
or "rational" as Pope's primal scenes are; again, how different this
Essay from that on Criticism with the latter's long concluding
account of the progress of literary learning. On the whole, the
poet of Man has steered clear of history, though he occasionally
plucks from the air some exemplary person, a Borgia or a Catiline,
to make a nonce point. The *Essay* is essentially ahistorical—Man's
"time a moment, and a point his space" (1.72); Pope's reasoning is
largely based on immediately verifiable observation of common
experience—"just to look about us" (1.4)—especially experience of
transience and decay, of the devil known as opposed to the devil
not known. Time's passing makes no difference in the human
condition: "Nero reigns a Titus, if he will" (II.198), the present
tense adding emphasis. History offers no certitude in the most
important matters:

> But still this world (so fitted for the knave)
> Contents us not. A better shall we have?
> A kingdom of the Just then let it be:
> But first consider how those Just agree.
> The good must merit God's peculiar care;
> But who, but God, can tell us who they are?
> One thinks on Calvin Heav'n's own spirit fell,
> Another deems him instrument of hell. . . .   (IV.131–38)

And God, needless to say, does not tell us, at least does not do so
directly, because he has implanted in us from creation the sense to

concentrate on more basic questions: what man can do, what society is, and what the limits are of each. Given such limits a society of the just cannot be perfectly attained.

This is the message of Pope's prehistory, which more than any passage in the poem offers some defense of the question begged at the beginning: there is a God of infinite wisdom who created the best possible world, a proposition indisputable because any alternative is unthinkable, has not been thought, or at least was not until humanity permitted itself to be corrupted: "The state of Nature was the reign of God" (III.148). How did man come to know God and the perfection of nature? He *does*: that is the main point. The prehistory assumes it, yet accounts for it too, providing separate, alternative explanations. At first the people may have regarded the patriarch as divine,

> 'Till drooping, sick'ning, dying, they began
> Whom they rever'd as God to mourn as Man:
> Then, looking up from sire to sire, explor'd
> One great first father, and that first ador'd.
> Or plain tradition that this All begun,
> Convey'd unbroken faith from sire to son,
> The worker from the work distinct was known,
> And simple Reason never sought but one:
> Ere Wit oblique had broke that steddy light,
> Man, like his Maker, saw that all was right. . . .   (III.223–32)

Induction and deduction, experience and tradition come together in Pope's most sustained apologetic passage, reason for the deist, authority for the fideist, and something for all the sects in between. Yet as Pope must have known, no amount of reasoning can finally instill faith, if faith is faith. Pope must rely on his own authority, in effect on his rhetoric.

Significantly, the apologetic passage occurs at the most auspicious moment, just after the holiest lines in the *Essay*, the *Essay's* revelation: Nature's speech. "The prosopopoeia is magnificent," wrote Joseph Warton;[4] susceptible men of the eighteenth century saw such a passage in higher relief than we, and with readier awe. It may be revealing to compare Nature's part here with old Diotima's in the *Symposium*, their functions are so similar. Like Pope, Socrates begins his speech with sharp criticism of his auditors, putting them on the defensive, opening a channel for his own superior answer to the question being debated. Then, instead of delivering the mystical answer himself, he aligns himself with his auditors as a fellow student, gathering them to him in a posture of receptive humility and introducing a person more authoritative than himself, sage Diotima. Upon entering the *Essay*, Pope's Nature quickly reveals herself to be religious as well as divine, with a reference to the "Creatures" man ought to imitate (III.172); as Pope says later, the virtuous man will look "thro' Nature, up to Nature's God" (IV.332). In Plato, the practicability of Diotima's advice is "proven" by Alcibiades and Socrates himself, whose various comments and actions show that Socrates has fully scaled the ladder of love. Pope accomplishes something of the same kind when Nature is found to speak in a pattern familiar to us from the earlier epistles, the conjunction of encouragement and scarification in an imperative strain we immediately recognize, though it is some time since the poet last spoke that way.

> Mark what unvary'd laws preserve each state,
> Laws wise as Nature, and as fix'd as Fate.
> In vain thy Reason finer webs shall draw,
> Entangle Justice in her net of Law,
> And right, too rigid, harden into wrong;
> Still for the strong too weak, the weak too strong.
> Yet go! and thus o'er all the creatures sway,

[4] *An Essay on the Genius and Writings of Pope*, II (London, 1782), 164. Compare Professor Mack's remarks, in the Twickenham Edition, about the "absence of Magnificence" in the poem (p. lxxiv).

Thus let the wiser make the rest obey,
And for those Arts mere Instinct could afford,
Be crown'd as Monarchs, or as Gods ador'd. (III.189–98)

The modulation in Pope's tone since he turned away from his reader toward the past distinguishes him from speaking Nature (he had not so distinguished himself from Pride in Epistle I), but upon reflection the reader finds that Nature and Pope are the same —not because he seems to be impersonating her but because, in manner and substance, from a perspective of some length, she independently corroborates what he has been saying to the submissive, now reverential candidate. As the poet says a little later, "Poet or Patriot, rose but to restore/ The Faith and Moral, Nature gave before" (III.285–86). In the *Essay* Pope has it both ways, at the risk of straining his readers' receptivity. In the epistles and satires concurrent with and subsequent to the *Essay,* he speaks less autocratically and, because he himself seems more receptive, he speaks too with easier credibility.

6. *Moral Essays:* Against Imitation

Horace, it may be recalled from *An Essay on Criticism,* "without Method *talks* us into Sense," and Heaven, to paraphrase the second *Moral Essay,* produced indefinably attractive Martha Blount by shaking all her sweet contradictory elements together. An equivalently free process may explain the organization, at least the order, of the four *Moral Essays:* two on analysis of characters male and female, two on the proper use of wealth. The series, if series it is, does meander—from an inventory of the obstacles to understanding particular persons, to a discourse (not, certainly, amoral) on architecture and gardening—and the poet leaps, as an essayist may: how abrupt, for example, is his reversion to the addressee, Cobham, at the end of the first epistle, the climax to nearly forty lines ridiculing seven characters who carried their delusions to the grave:

> And you! brave COBHAM, to the latest breath
> Shall feel your ruling passion strong in death:
> Such in those moments as in all the past,
> "Oh, save my Country, Heav'n!" shall be your last.

Yet the four poems may have an unobtrusive order. Pope did number them in a sequence different from that of their composi-

tion or publication, presumably doing so not just to keep track of
them, and he designed them to form part of the large philosophical work that, if completed, would have elaborated *An Essay on
Man.* In this chapter I shall trace what I take to be the cumulative
action of the series, arguing that the poems together represent an
ethical enquiry of considerable effort, resourcefulness, and
maturity.

That—in context—gratuitous compliment to Cobham points
to another question: why in epistles designedly moral, in essays
denominated "Ethic,"[1] a reader encounters so few characters who
are good. Portraits by the dozen fill the series, usually developed

---

[1] F. W. Bateson, the Twickenham editor, notes that Warburton, not Pope,
named them *Moral Essays.* Pope called them *Ethic Epistles,* later simply *Epistles to
Several Persons.* See Vol. III-ii: *Epistles to Several Persons (Moral Essays)* (2d ed.;
London, 1961), pp. v, xiv*n.* The sequential order of the epistles or essays was
established in the first collected edition (1735), and in the Advertisement to the
last edition Pope supervised (1744) he explained that the four essays were "detached portions" of a projected series on "Ethics, or practical Morality" to have
been added to *An Essay on Man,* relating to the fourth epistle of that work, had he
completed the Magnum Opus he contemplated; Pope says too that *Moral Essays*
I-II were to be the "introductory part" (Bateson, pp. xix-xx). Samuel Johnson
scoffs at William Warburton's effort (in the Commentary to the *Essays* as printed
in the *Works* of 1751, Vol. III) "to find a train of thought which was never in the
writer's head" (Pope," *Lives of the English Poets,* ed. George Birkbeck Hill [Oxford,
1905], III, 245)—a stricture I hope inapplicable to my much more general sketch.
Johnson erroneously thought that Warburton numbered the *Essays;* Warburton
did help Pope prepare the edition of 1744, but if Warburton had a hand in the
Advertisement, I think it odd that he allowed *Essays* III-IV to pass as merely "detached portions," since he later gave such detailed attention to their possible re-
latedness. Pope had much earlier claimed more in a letter to Swift of February,
1733, asserting a "plain connexion" between *Essays* III and IV if read in that order,
"in the order just contrary to that they were published in" (*Correspondence,* ed.
George Sherburn [5 vols.; Oxford, 1956], III, 348, where a footnote mistakenly
says Pope "is thinking of his four 'Moral Essays'"; only *Essays* III-IV had been published at the time). In the present chapter my most conspicuous leap is across
the gap between *Essays* II and III, not perhaps a very long leap considering Pope's
bringing up the topic of riches at the end of the former, the last of the four to be
published.

in accordance with Pope's pet theory of the "ruling passion," nearly all of them dissections of fools and/or knaves. When the good do appear they bear elusive characters, suggesting, as seems true, that the device of a ruling passion particularly suits diagnostic rather than merely descriptive purposes. Cobham, Bathurst, Burlington, the noble noblemen of Epistles I, III, and IV, respectively, go all but undescribed though they clearly represent norms of good conduct; Martha Blount, the *Lady* of Epistle II, defies definition; the Man of Ross, in the *Epistle to Bathurst*, remains a remote, hallowed figure known, like the God of nature, through his works. Moreover, all but one of Pope's characters, negative and positive, are decidedly static; only Balaam, in the third epistle, changes while Pope describes him, and his motion proves evil. If men may move themselves toward goodness, and that they may seems the basic rationale of poems such as these, Pope nowhere reveals it happening. A more inert set of portraits would be hard to find outside a museum, yet the *Essays*, as I shall try to show, are seriously concerned with the dynamics of goodness as well as with moral or moralistic warnings about the consequences of evil.

As an heir not just of the classics but of Locke, Pope recognized that ethics requires a psychology, that prescription must proceed from description—description excluding no potential sources. That is the point of the opening lines in the *Epistle to Cobham:* somehow the philosopher must achieve a balance, relying upon both his own observations and the observations of others, upon experience and upon learning, so as to attain maximum knowledge and objectivity. In *An Essay on Man* Pope had somewhat peremptorily set forth aprioristic principles. Here he will speak more moderately, less lawgiver than enquirer. Here the ethician will reveal the psychologist, the researcher will trot out his case histories, and here will be demonstrated, in a matter-of-fact way, the practicability of moral philosophy. Evidently Pope was not content to parade examples of vices as a moral theologian might line up Seven Deadly Sinners. He wished or presumed also to locate the natural root of morality, the "spring of action" (*Moral Essays*, I.42), the decisive first cause of good and evil behavior and to account for it psychologically, not theologically, so as to explain the mechanism of good and evil.

It was, to Pope, a crucial matter, for though he never ceased to believe in human freedom—"Nero reigns a Titus, if he will" (*An Essay on Man*, II.198)—he believed against the tide of his philosophical system, which recurrently swells with determinism of one sort or another; for example:

> Who knows but he, whose hand the light'ning forms,
> Who heaves old Ocean, and who wings the storms,
> Pours fierce Ambition in a Cæsar's mind,
> Or turns young Ammon loose to scourge mankind?
>
> (*An Essay on Man*, I.157–60)

Whether, as here, the determinant is a direct divine intervention or simply an element in the optimal order of the universe (Pope's more systematic explanation), hardly matters. The determinant denies freedom. Yet "Reason the byass turns to good from ill" (*An Essay on Man*, II.197) so that Nero may become virtuous with the aid of reason and will power. How? How, in Pope's own terms, shall a man learn to rule his own ruling passion?

As described in *An Essay on Man*, the ruling passion is originally peccant, "the Mind's disease" (II.138), but since it is *the* driving force in human nature, the source of man's energy, it will not be extirpated, balked, or ignored. If a man is to become virtuous he must do so by rational direction of its energy: "The surest Virtues thus from Passions shoot" (II.183)—an appealing, constructive description of human nature, suitable to the purposes of a Freud: speaking to Cobham on the relation of dreams to experience,

Pope comments: "Something as dim to our internal view,/ Is thus, perhaps, the cause of most we do" (I.49–50). But how, the problem remains, does a man disengage his reason from the power of a sovereign passion, and how muster the energy to exert guidance upon the passion? Whence, if not from the passion, does the force of reason come? If reason is a chart and passion the wind (II.108), what activates the hand on the tiller? At the end of his account of the ruling passion in *An Essay on Man* Pope asks the question himself but answers it much too summarily: "What shall divide? The God within the mind" (II.204).[2] His eye less on ethics than on theodicy, he concentrates there upon vindicating the general goodness of the universe, a goodness finally unaffected by what men do, evil inevitably resulting in good. He does not theologize about the deity in the mind. The answer, of course, invariably in all ethics, is to be found in personal autonomy based on knowledge of the self in its circumstances, an answer validated by the quality of that knowledge. If the *Moral Essays* represent a search for such knowledge and independent power, the quest proves circular but not disenabling.

[2] As ever, Maynard Mack writes perceptively and sympathetically of this crux in Pope's philosophy, especially in the Introduction to the Twickenham Edition of *An Essay on Man;* III-i (London, 1950), xxxviii, xli–xlii. In the notes to *Epistle* II he appositely quotes from the *Imitations of Horace, Ep.* II.ii.278–83, which includes reference to "That God of Nature, who, within us still,/ Inclines our Action, not constrains our Will." If Pope could not fully reconcile such statements with each other, he at least had the sense and honesty to juxtapose them, in doing so upholding modern theory—as a blunt passage from Ernst Cassirer makes plain: "The psychology and ethics of the seventeenth century are in the main based on this conception of the affects as 'perturbations of the mind' *(perturbationes animi)*. Only that action has ethical value which overcomes these disturbances, which illustrates the triumph of the active over the passive part of the soul, of reason over the passions. This Stoic view not merely dominates the philosophy of the seventeenth century, but it permeates the intellectual life of the age in general. On this point Descartes' teaching agrees with that of Corneille. The rule of the

"Yes, you despise the man to Books confin'd," Pope begins the first essay. For many in the eighteenth and preceding centuries, the main purpose of reading was to build up a fund of vicarious experience for moral ends. Asked why a person should read, Pope told Joseph Spence "to make myself and others better." Recommending the study of history, Pope went on to describe his manner of pursuing it: "I would mark down: 'on such an occasion the people concerned proceeded in such a manner; it was evidently wrong and had a very ill effect; a statesman therefore should avoid it in a like case.' Such a one did good or got an honest reputation by such an action: I would mark it down in order to imitate it where I had an opportunity." Thus Nero would begin by reading about a Titus. Yet Pope knew, as he had said in the *Essay on Criticism*, that men can "through *Imitation* err," and, as much of the first *Moral Essay* reveals, he knew also how difficult it was to fathom the motivation of historical figures. On another occasion late in his life he remarked to Spence: "Facts in ancient history are not very instructive now; the principles of acting vary so often and so greatly. The actions of a great man were quite different even in

---

rational will over all desires of sense, over appetites and passions, proclaims and expresses the freedom of man. The eighteenth century advances beyond this negative characterization and evaluation of the affects. It looks upon the affects not as a mere obstacle, but seeks to show that they are the original and indispensable impulse of all the operations of the mind" (*The Philosophy of the Enlightenment*, tr. Fritz C. A. Koelln and James P. Pettegrove [Princeton, 1951], pp. 105–6). For a more elaborate, qualified account of the history of this question in and just preceding Pope's time—an account incorporating the relatively benign view of the passions which derived from "traditional Peripatetic ethics so frequently accepted by Christian moralists in the seventeenth and early eighteenth centuries"—see Bertrand A. Goldgar, "Pope's Theory of the Passions: The Background of Epistle II of the *Essay on Man*," *PQ*, XLI (1962), 730–43, esp. p. 735; and also Douglas H. White, *Pope and the Context of Controversy: The Manipulation of Ideas in "An Essay on Man"* (Chicago, 1970), esp. p. 128; on pp. 139–42 White explicates the card-gale passage, concluding that "probably the soul is the pilot in this metaphor."

Scipio's and Julius Caesar's times."[3] Or, as he remarked in the *Epistle to Cobham*, "That very Caesar, born in Scipio's days,/ Had aim'd, like him, by Chastity at praise" (ll. 216–17).

The first epistle, Pope's *Apology for Raymond Sebond*, does not take him very far beyond *An Essay on Man*. Defending himself against the peer's impetuous disdain for the bookish man, he lengthily enumerates the various fallible means of comprehending human behavior, settling finally but unenthusiastically upon the ruling passion, which is redefined. Here is a key, but as he describes it the key seems to unlock only the doors of sepulchers: Wharton, the lecherous clergyman, gluttonous Helluo, the miserly crone, Narcissa, . . . avaricious Euclio—an unrelieved series of wretches hardened and unregenerate, rigidly their twisted selves even unto death, except for Cobham and the four final lines of compliment upon his unexplained passion of patriotism. The second epistle continues in this vein: portraits of Rufa, Sappho, Silia, Papillia, Narcissa (again) . . . climaxed by a profile of indescribable Martha Blount, except for Cobham the first attractive person encountered in the *Essays*. Some women have a ruling passion, either love of pleasure or love of sovereignty. Not Martha, however; she is a happy jumble of qualities: Heaven "Shakes all together, and produces—You" (l. 280). That is what she is, herself, and that is—mysteriously—how she got that way. Heaven

[3] Joseph Spence, *Observations, Anecdotes, and Characters of Books and Men Collected from Conversation*, ed. James M. Osborn (2 vols.; Oxford, 1966), I, 241. Osborn and Bateson note that the same example occurs in the *Epistle to Cobham*. Apropos of this point and the general theme of this chapter, I might recall Johnson's opinion that the first two *Moral Essays* "are the product of diligent speculation upon human life" ("Pope," III, 248) and Johnson's general opinion of Pope's intellectual power: "His frequent references to history, his allusions to various kinds of knowledge, and his images selected from art and nature, with his observations on the operations of the mind and the modes of life, shew an intelligence perpetually on the wing, excursive, vigorous, and diligent, eager to pursue knowledge, and attentive to retain it" (III, 216).

made her beautiful "but deny'd the Pelf/ Which buys your sex a Tyrant o'er itself" (ll. 287–88). The virtue of Martha is not entirely *sui generis.* Had she been rich she might, or would probably, have become corrupt.

The opening lines of Epistle III pursue the theme of money's tyranny:

> Who shall decide, when Doctors disagree,
> And soundest Casuists doubt, like you and me?
> You hold the word, from Jove to Momus giv'n,
> That Man was made the standing jest of Heav'n;
> And Gold but sent to keep the fools in play,
> For some to heap, and some to throw away.
> But I, who think more highly of our kind,
> (And surely, Heav'n and I are of a mind)
> Opine, that Nature, as in duty bound,
> Deep hid the shining mischief under ground:
> But when by Man's audacious labour won,
> Flam'd forth this rival to, its Sire, the Sun,
> Then careful Heav'n supply'd two sorts of Men,
> To squander these, and those to hide agen.
> Like Doctors thus, when much dispute has past,
> We find our tenets just the same at last.

Opposing Bathurst's cynical theory with its pagan reference to Jove, Pope momentarily and somewhat playfully vindicates Christianity with a reference to Heaven, the God of which tried to keep gold from men, in vain. The precious stuff unearthed, Pope holds, God supplied men designed to—determined to—deal with it excessively by either elimination or retention. Money is the immediate determinant of human action. *All* human action? The lines that follow seem to say just that; Bathurst would therefore repudiate not just gold but the whole venal world (l. 80), and what Pope says directly afterward would tend to bear him out: the poet extends his catalogue of vicious and deluded characters until:

"All this is madness," cries a sober sage:
But who, my friend, has reason in his rage?
   "The ruling Passion, be it what it will,
"The ruling Passion conquers Reason still."
Less mad the wildest whimsey we can frame,
Than ev'n that Passion, if it has no Aim;
For tho' such motives Folly you may call,
The Folly's greater to have none at all.
   Hear then the truth: " 'Tis Heav'n each Passion sends,
"And diff'rent men directs to diff'rent ends.
"Extremes in Nature equal good produce,
"Extremes in Man concur to gen'ral use."
Ask we what makes one keep, and one bestow?
That Pow'ʀ who bids the Ocean ebb and flow,
Bids seed-time, harvest, equal course maintain,
Thro' reconcil'd extremes of drought and rain,
Builds Life on Death, on Change Duration founds,
And gives th' eternal wheels to know their rounds.   (ll. 153–70)

—lines finally as deterministic as those I have quoted above from
An Essay on Man, about the power of the hand which "heaves old
Ocean." Here, speaking to Bathurst, the Essayist on Man recalls
readers to the great general principle of his long general poem:
the miser and the prodigal, as the ensuing lines proclaim, do
ultimately though unintentionally produce good. But comforting
as these thoughts may be in the long perspective of *An Essay on
Man*, they seem inadequate to the needs of the Moral Essayist,
the relentless practical enquirer. Pope is here determined (in one
sense or the other) to find a means for man to participate and
choose, to take his proper part, in what is otherwise an inexorable
cosmic process (comparably, a poet might wish to write in a given
genre without agreeing to write exactly as the genre seems to
require); Pope is not just determined, he is passionately intent.
In lines more forceful than any yet heard in this series of epistles,
with an energy apparent in the most unconversational periodicity
and culminating enjambment, Pope cries, declaims:

> The Sense to value Riches, with the Art
> T' enjoy them, and the Virtue to impart,
> Not meanly, nor ambitiously pursu'd,
> Not sunk by sloth, nor rais'd by servitude;
> To balance Fortune by a just expence,
> Join with Oeconomy, Magnificence;
> With Splendor, Charity; with Plenty, Health;
> Oh teach us, BATHURST! yet unspoil'd by wealth!
> That secret rare, between th' extremes to move
> Of mad Good-nature, and of mean Self-love.   (ll. 219–28)

For man must somehow accept the world God made and yet seek to "Mend Fortune's fault" (l. 232), a paradox like that involved in ruling a ruling passion. The cosmic question has a microcosmic variant.

If Bathurst has the answer, however, Pope does not give it to his readers. He simply praises Bathurst for adherence to a virtually unparticularized golden mean—then in some detail begins to discourse on an exemplary person of the highest virtue, the Man of Ross, only the second such person to be described in the whole series. Martha, the other, is inimitably her contradictory self; the Man of Ross, a magnificent philanthropist on a small budget, may provide a more practical model, yet he is seen chiefly in his works, a presence but remote. What motivated him? What possessed him to behave so nobly? The mystery remains, to be followed in this poem by more particular, deprecatory portraits: of Villiers and of Balaam, the fortunate Job who, prey to fortune, ends cursing God. The first kinetic portrait in the whole series, that of Balaam tends only to reiterate the deterministic power of money; the third essay ends where it began.

Weak Balaam wilts before our eyes. To this point we have been given innumerable portraits of the statically bad and—a few—of the unswervingly good, as well as a restatement of the optimist determinism of *An Essay on Man*, as well, moreover, as a prayer to an allegedly good man for guidance—unanswered. One might

ask, with Johnson of *The Vanity of Human Wishes,* "Must helpless
man, in ignorance sedate,/ Roll darkling down the torrent of his
fate?" Johnson will counsel resignation and prayer. Pope the
psychologist begins to hold forth, in the final epistle, on—architecture and gardening! But here there occurs a definite development in the series, for whereas Bathurst had been asked for
guidance, Burlington is extolled for providing it: "You show us,
Rome was glorious, not profuse,/ And pompous buildings once
were things of Use"—as much as it can be provided: "Yet shall
(my Lord) your just, your noble rules/ Fill half the land with
Imitating Fools." Why?—for a reason given at the beginning of
this epistle, which carries forward the miser-prodigal dichotomy
and explains it with the remark that the unbalanced person,
whatever his excess, acts "Not for himself." Later lines expand the
notion:

> Oft have you hinted to your brother Peer,
> A certain truth, which many buy too dear:
> Something there is more needful than Expence,
> And something previous ev'n to Taste—'tis Sense:
> Good Sense, which only is the gift of Heav'n,
> And tho' no science, fairly worth the sev'n:
> A Light, which in yourself you must perceive;
> Jones and Le Nôtre have it not to give.
>   To build, to plant, whatever you intend,
> To rear the Column, or the Arch to bend,
> To swell the Terras, or to sink the Grot;
> In all, let Nature never be forgot.
> But treat the Goddess like a modest fair,
> Nor over-dress, nor leave her wholly bare;
> Let not each beauty ev'ry where be spy'd,
> Where half the skill is decently to hide.
> He gains all points, who pleasingly confounds,
> Surprizes, varies, and conceals the Bounds.
>   Consult the Genius of the Place in all. . . .   (ll. 39–57)

Earler, before drawing Martha's portrait in the second epistle, Pope praised the ideal woman in words that Clarissa might have spoken in *The Rape of the Lock:* she, ideal she, "Lets Fops and Fortune fly which way they will;/ Disdains all loss of Tickets, or Codille" (ll. 265–66). Here his manner suggests that, addressing Burlington, he is rewriting the *Essay on Criticism* in behalf of gardening.[4] Before the poem ends, after the long cautionary description of Timon—climaxed with rationalization once more from *An Essay on Man:* the spendthrift's folly feeds the poor— Pope will recall the strains of *Windsor-Forest* while praising that man "Whose rising Forests, not for pride or show,/ But future Buildings, future Navies grow" (ll. 187–88); he goes on to encourage Burlington as he did Granville years before.

The more things have changed through twenty years of poeticizing, the more they have remained the same, it seems, yet perhaps not entirely so. The ruling passion, mentioned frequently throughout the first three epistles, goes unnoticed here. Man does, Pope realized, have obscure, characterizing drives and an intelligence with which, all being equal or well, to begin to understand and direct them. But that being established he reached the end of his investigative tether. He was not to be remembered as a psychologist, though he had attempted to plumb human motivation: first describing the difficulties, then isolating types of character (and seemingly, to judge by results, finding illness easier to describe than health), then appealing for guidance, finally recognizing, at least proclaiming, that guidance in any significant human activity cannot usurp the claims and responsibilities of the self or compensate entirely for its deficiencies. Whatever the source, sense remains "A Light, which in yourself you must

[4] As James E. Wellington remarks in the Introduction to his edition of *Epistles to Several Persons (Moral Essays)* (University of Miami Critical Studies, No. 2; Coral Gables, 1963), pp. 75–76.

perceive;/ Jones and Le Nôtre have it not to give," and sense,
paltry as it sometimes is, in the last analysis remains the individual's final guide, philosopher, friend, and exemplar, in morals as
well as in gardening.

Pope emerges from the four epistles bearing sentiments which,
if reduced to a slogan, sound like the mouthings of Polonius. The
difference is, Pope has represented himself as working through
to his position, attending to psychology, history, ethics; consulting
friends and patrons; balancing, or at least juxtaposing, common
sense with theodicy; asking, arguing, agreeing, teaching, ob-
serving—doing, in effect, everything a man can do to achieve
moral wisdom and, more to the point, exhibiting his own positive
morality in the course of—by—doing it. The resources of moral
judgment are available; throughout the series Pope describes and
employs them, in a manner less autocratic, more enquiring and
congenial than that of *An Essay on Man.* Given models good and
bad, characters proximate, remote, and ideal, given rules, a man
remains or becomes "Sole judge of Truth." He realizes it, fully
and responsibly for himself, when he has pursued all possible aids
to their ends and found himself alone, independent, in a position
to will. Nero could not, after all, have become Titus but might
have made himself a decent Nero. The uniqueness of the ruling
passion finds its complement in the power a man must generate
upon recognizing his own distinctness, from a study of negative
exemplars, certainly, but also from analysis of good people. The
better Job of the *Essays* is the poet who patiently develops and
holds to his own moral vision even when, as in the epistles to Cobham and Bathurst, especially, it differs from that of his friends.

In the Horatian imitations, with communicable pleasure, Pope
tends to dwell on meetings less trying than these.

7. Imitations of Horace: Oral Literature

The Horace who speaks in his own satires and epistles is, on the whole, an enviable figure, at home in the world, fulfilled, satisfied, a person integrated intellectually, emotionally, socially—a man next to whom the Pope of the *Imitations*, even to readers unfamiliar with the relevant biography, may recall that proberb of Blake's in *The Marriage of Heaven and Hell:* "Prudence is a rich ugly old maid courted by Incapacity." Piddling on broccoli, tending his old mother and his infirm self, Pope may seem pitiable enough to breed suspicions that in his eyes vice is abhorrent partially because it can be so strenuous. In this connection it is surprising that Pope translated *Satires* i.ii, the bawdy "Sober Advice," but not that he pretended someone else had written it. He is not the epicurean Horace was; yet as I hope to show in the following pages, the satires have warmth as well as brilliance, a dynamic distinguishable from bitterness—and not simply stated but repeatedly enacted and implied.

To some extent Pope's power shines in the drama of the *Imitations*, a quality he valued more highly than Horace did, to judge by the fact that most of Horace's pieces are much less dramatic, none more, than the two satires of the series that Pope wrote entirely on his own: the *Epistle to Dr. Arbuthnot* (called the prologue by William Warburton, Pope's editor, perhaps with the poet's approval) and the *Epilogue to the Satires*. The latter is conventionally dramatic, consisting of two outright dialogues; but *Arbuthnot* is subtler, for the *adversarius* has minimal significance. The drama lies in the monologue, an adventure in self-discovery.

Useful as it is to distinguish the voices Pope employs, the meat of his art is in the transitions between them: in *Arbuthnot*, the way in which Pope, apparently rambling, composes not just a poem but also himself, developing from the harried, frantic little man who seeks sanctuary in the opening lines to the resolute exponent of virtue who speaks calmly at the end. What accounts for the change? Not, certainly, anything Arbuthnot says; the change proceeds from within the poet, the result of an intensive examination of himself and his society. Social in manner as well as theme, the poem rises through a series of comparisons: how did they—hangers-on and enemies—treat me? how did I treat them? Why did I write, publish? Why do they? Passages of autobiography alternate with passages of history throughout the first half of the poem, where it is established that Pope was born to write, published because distinguished friends urged him to, heeded sensible criticism and ignored or suffered foolish (all these circumstances so patently natural and good, especially when compared with those of other poets)—and even, far from rejoicing in the disabilities of his rival, Atticus, could weep over them. Every word of Addison's portrait gains life from comparisons and contrasts, explicit and hinted, with what Pope says about his own behavior: Atticus, for example, bears "like the *Turk*, no brother near the throne," though encouraging flatterers, while Pope seeks "no homage from the Race that write;/ I kept, like *Asian* Monarchs, from their sight" (ll. 198, 219–20);

but the cross-references are too clear to require exhaustive dem-
onstration. The first 260 lines of the poem, focused on the past
and culminating in the portrait of Bufo, the tasteless patron,
constitute a persuasively righteous valediction to the literary
society from which Pope has sequestered himself, upon which
John has closed the door. "Oh let me live my own! and die so
too!" "Heav'ns! was I born for nothing but to write?" (ll. 261,
272). It looks as if he shall lay down his pen forever, and, considering what he says he has suffered, he can hardly be blamed.

Yet a few lines later Pope has begun a bold satiric manifesto
followed by a declaration of war upon Sporus—why? The manifesto concentrates upon not the folly of Pope's enemies but the
actual harm they do: lies and libels, detraction, neglect, betrayal.
That fraud *has* social consequences of a baneful kind, that decep-
tion injures others besides the deluded, is a theme that begins
to sound loudly as the portrait of Bufo comes to a close: the
patron "help'd to starve" Dryden (l. 248); also,

> Blest be the *Great!* for those they take away,
> And those they left me—For they left me GAY,
> Left me to see neglected Genius bloom,
> Neglected die! and tell it on his Tomb;
> Of all thy blameless Life the sole Return
> My Verse, and QUEENSB'RY weeping o'er thy Urn!   (ll. 255–60)

The antisocial man, particularly the diabolical Sporus, must be
opposed, not simply ignored; the good man, no matter what he
has suffered, cannot immure himself from his responsibilities,
though he must protect himself as well as he can. "Not Fortune's
Worshipper, nor Fashion's Fool . . ." (l. 334); thus begins a
kind of epitaph upon himself, the complete social man—successfully both aloof and engaged—sustained by self-knowledge,

history, and a grasp of morals and manners, strengthened by experience of his family and friends. With a group portrait— Pope aiding his mother, Arbuthnot aiding Pope—the poem ends as the poet manfully looks to the future. Set against this picture, the *Epilogue*, with its bereft, finally alienated poet, reveals the fullness of gloom.

None of Pope's other satires presents so complete a change in the speaker, as is fitting because he needs to be created only once. His rancor, *Arbuthnot* shows, is the verso of his love, not simply the issue of his spleen: his love of rectitude (abstractly of Virtue, concretely of exemplary human beings), of his family and friends, and of conditions in which these things come together. More than any other, that situation, the imagined setting for Pope's satire and Horace's, is a dinner party, in Latin a *cena*. *Sermones*, Horace's word for his satires, denotes conversation; in the fifth epistle of his first book he invites Torquatus to dinner, promising a summer night prolonged in genial talk (ll. 10-11); *Fecundi calices quem non fecere disertum?* (l. 19). Elsewhere, defending his writing of satire, he recalls the golden past and his predecessor in satire, Lucilius: "What! when Lucilius first dared to compose poems after this kind, and to strip off the skin with which each strutted all bedecked before the eyes of men, though foul within, was Laelius offended at his wit, or he who took his well-earned name from conquered Carthage? Or were they hurt because Metellus was smitten, and Lupus buried under a shower of lampooning verses? Yet he laid hold upon the leaders of the people, and upon the people in their tribes, kindly in fact only to Virtue and her friends. Nay, when virtuous Scipio and the wise and gentle Laelius withdrew into privacy from the throng and theatre of life, they would turn to folly, and flinging off restraint would indulge with him in sport while their dish of herbs was on the boil"

(*Sat.* II.i.62–74).[1] As is well known, the word *satura* implies a bowl of mixed food. The bubbling pot, the generous amphora are the fuel for the satirist's fire. When Horace writes of a conversation he has had on the road, away from the table, he is not simply representing it—he is presenting it to his auditors, and what place more appropriate than the convivial board, surrounded by intimates at their ease?

Nor, among such men, will the conversation be confined to bitter gossip. In the sixth satire of the second book, Horace describes another dinner, this time regretting that he must be in Rome and not back on the farm: "O when shall beans, brethren of Pythagoras, be served me, and with them greens well larded with fat bacon! O nights and feasts divine! When before my own Lar we dine, my friends and I, and feed the saucy slaves from the barely tasted dishes. Each guest, as is his fancy, drains cups big or small, not bound by crazy laws, whether one can stand strong bumpers in gallant style, or with mild cups mellows more to his

---

[1] Tr. H. Rushton Fairclough, *Horace: Satires, Epistles and Ars Poetica* (Loeb Classical Library; Cambridge, Mass., 1929). In his preliminary note to *Sat.* II. viii Fairclough remarks that Lucilius, who transmitted the Greek tradition of the δεῖπνον to Latin satire, "wrote at least five satires on banquets" (p. 237). John Butt, in the introduction to the *Imitations* in the Twickenham Edition, Vol. IV, recalls Pope's telling Spence "that he had imitated more than are printed, mentioning in particular the fourth satire of the second book" ([2d ed.; London, 1953], p. xxxvi). In *Sat.* II. iv an amused Horace listens to a friend's description of a lecture on cookery. The eating motif has importance in other poems of Pope, particularly the *Moral Essays* and *The Dunciad* (especially IV.549–64 of the latter, the ghastly gluttons' Mass); see Patricia Meyer Spacks, *An Argument of Images: The Poetry of Alexander Pope* (Cambridge, Mass., 1971), pp. 117–21, for a discriminating account of the function of eating here and elsewhere in *The Dunciad*. My chapter may owe something to Geoffrey Tillotson's *Pope and Human Nature* (Oxford, 1958), p. 29, where Boswell's definition of man is quoted, "a Cooking Animal," and Burke's approving reply: "Your definition is good, . . . and now I see the full force of the common proverb, 'There is *reason* in roasting of eggs.'"

liking. And so begins a chat, not about other men's homes and
estates, nor whether Lepos dances well or ill; but we discuss
matters which concern us more, and of which it is harmful to
be in ignorance—whether wealth or virtue makes men happy,
whether self-interest or uprightness leads us to friendship, what
is the nature of the good and what is its highest form (ll. 63–76).
High subjects indeed, but preachment is not foreign to the *sermo*,
and one must not take Horace's words too literally: three lines
later and his neighbor Cervius begins a fable, that of the Country
Mouse and the City Mouse, to instruct another of the company
who has praised the wealth of Arellius without considering the
anxieties that attend it. "Other men's . . . estates" do come up.
The satiric conversation following dinner will hurt with wit
what it heals with morals.

Both passages have their counterparts in Pope. He plays down
the mischief of Lucilius, Scipio, and Laelius, reducing Horace's
scene to the lines:

> There, my Retreat the best Companions grace,
> Chiefs, out of War, and Statesmen, out of Place.
> There *St. John* mingles with my friendly Bowl,
> The Feast of Reason and the Flow of Soul. . . .   (*Sat.* ii.i.125–28)

(The Earl of Peterborough, the Scipio of the scene, busies himself
in the garden, whence dinner is procured.) But the friendly bowl,
the fountain of chatter and philosophy, gains prominence here
because of some lines that precede the passage, lines in a context
of drinking. "I love to pour out all myself," Pope confesses (the
poet as decanter),

>   as plain
> As downright *Shippen,* or as old *Montagne.*
> In them, as certain to be lov'd as seen,
> The Soul stood forth, nor kept a Thought within;

In me what Spots (for Spots I have) appear,
Will prove at least the Medium must be clear.
In this impartial Glass, my Muse intends
Fair to expose myself, my Foes, my Friends. . . .   (ll. 51–58)

The lines Pope quite fittingly contributed to Swift's chatty
Imitation of *Satires* II.vi include a version, in unstately tetrameters,
of the country dinner party Horace and Pope delighted in. And
to be sure, Pope says the subjects discussed are those sober philosophical questions enumerated by Horace. But the scene, as Pope
describes it, is more *cena* than symposium:

O charming Noons! and Nights divine!
Or when I sup, or when I dine,
My Friends above, my Folks below,
Chatting and laughing all-a-row,
The Beans and Bacon set before 'em,
The Grace-cup serv'd with all decorum:
Each willing to be pleas'd, and please,
And even the very Dogs at ease!   (ll. 133–40)

Table-talk is represented in other places through the *Imitations;*
most, however, in Pope's paraphrase of *Satires* II.ii, which begins
with "Bethel's Sermon"—all about eating and drinking moderately but zestfully. The sermon finished, Pope applies it to himself with happy results, describing the cheerfulness of his un-
ostentatious, wholesome board surrounded by good-natured
visitors:

Content with little, I can piddle here
On Broccoli and mutton, round the year;
But ancient friends, (tho' poor, or out of play)
That touch my Bell, I cannot turn away.
'Tis true, no Turbots dignify my boards,
But gudgeons, flounders, what my Thames affords,
To Hounslow-heath I point, and Bansted-down,

Thence comes your mutton, and these chicks my own:
From yon old wallnut-tree a show'r shall fall;
And grapes, long-lingring on my only wall,
And figs, from standard and Espalier join:
The dev'l is in you if you cannot dine.
Then chearful healths (your Mistress shall have place)
And, what's more rare, a Poet shall say *Grace*.   (ll. 137–50)

More than Horace, too, Pope dramatizes the scene, realizing the
dinner party. The Roman, after a short introduction spoken by
himself, is content to quote his authority, Ofellus, throughout
all but a few lines of the rest of the poem. Pope's quotation from
Bethel, however, takes up just two-thirds of the imitation, after
which the English poet describes the manner in which his own
habits illustrate Bethel's maxims. If he errs, he does so on the
side of generosity and good-living—as he suggests as early as the
third line of the poem:

What, and how great, the Virtue and the Art
To live on little with a chearful heart,
(A Doctrine sage, but truly none of mine)
Lets talk, my friends, but talk before we dine. . . .   (ll. 1–4)

Horace's equivalent of the third line simply gives credit to Ofellus
(Nec meus hic Sermo, sed quem praecepit Ofellus). Pope's "truly"
stresses the point: Pope is dissociating himself somewhat from
Bethel, not simply distinguishing Bethel's thoughts from his own;
Spartan, declamatory Bethel has made no mention of conviviality,
of Pope's "chearful healths." And that the occasion of Pope's
satire is indeed a party seems demonstrated by several lines late
in the poem, lines with no precedent in Horace:

                    . . . My father's house is gone;
I'll hire another's, is not that my own,
And yours my friends? thro' whose free-opening gate
None comes too early, none departs too late;
(For I, who hold sage Homer's rule the best,

Welcome the coming, speed the going guest.)
"Pray heav'n it last! (cries Swift) as you go on;
"I wish to God this house had been your own:
"Pity! to build, without a son or wife:
"Why, you'll enjoy it only all your life."—
Well, if the Use be mine can it concern one
Whether the Name belong to Pope or Vernon?
What's *Property?* dear Swift! (ll. 155–67)

This is living: a dinner with Pope and Swift chaffing, sparkling together in company. How much more appealing than a walk in the fields with Bolingbroke, this scene of friends "Chatting and laughing all-a-row," of Pope pouring himself out plain. And what an improvement upon Horace, this dramatic realization of the dinner party.

Satire's mixed bowl is to be found on the dinner table. The *Epistle to Augustus*, more formal than the satires, has few direct references to eating, hardly a subject to set before a king. Yet in its elevated way it makes the argument more explicitly than any of the satires when it provides an etiology of the genre, another primal scene of the sort found in *An Essay on Man*, iii.

Our rural Ancestors, with little blest,
Patient of labour when the end was rest,
Indulg'd the day that housed their annual grain,
With feasts, and off'rings, and a thankful strain:
The joy their wives, their sons, and servants share,
Ease of their toil, and part'ners of their care:
The laugh, the jest, attendants on the bowl,
Smooth'd ev'ry brow, and open'd ev'ry soul:
With growing years the pleasing Licence grew,
And Taunts alternate innocently flew.
But Times currupt, and Nature, ill-inclined,
Produc'd the point that left a sting behind;
Till friend with friend, and families at strife,
Triumphant Malice rag'd thro' private life.
Who felt the wrong, or fear'd it, took th' alarm,

> Appeal'd to Law, and Justice lent her arm.
> At length, by wholesom dread of statutes bound,
> The Poets learn'd to please, and not to wound:
> Most warp'd to Flatt'ry's side; but some, more nice,
> Preserv'd the freedom, and forbore the vice.
> Hence Satire arose, that just the medium hit,
> And heals with Morals what it hurts with Wit.   (ll. 241–62)

Gastronomic references in the *Imitations* could be multiplied indefinitely. In *Epistles*, ii.ii, for example, Pope represents himself as a kind of literary chef; at least, host, the character he claims elsewhere.

> But after all, what wou'd you have me do?
> When out of twenty I can please not two;
> When this Heroicks only deigns to praise,
> Sharp Satire that, and that Pindaric lays?
> One likes the Pheasant's wing, and one the leg;
> The Vulgar boil, the Learned roast an Egg;
> Hard Task! to hit the Palate of such Guests,
> When Oldfield loves, what Dartineuf detests.   (ll. 80–87)

But there is little reason to multiply the references, except to indicate their relevance to other subjects of importance in this group of poems. The metaphor of consumption has clear applicability to parasitism—and of course to sexual hunger—"Some win rich Widows by their Chine and Brawn" (*Ep.* i.i.131); prodigality:

> All Worldly's Hens, nay Partridge, sold to town,
> His Ven'son too, a Guinea makes your own:
> He bought at thousands, what with better wit
> You purchase as you want, and bit by bit. . . .   (*Ep.* ii.ii.234–37)

hypocrisy: "Nor one that Temperance advance,/ Cramm'd to the throat with Ortolans" (*Ep.* i.vii.61–62); greed: "And Lands and Tenements go down her Throat" (*Sat.* i.ii.14); pride: "When sharp with Hunger, scorn you to be fed,/ Except on *Pea-Chicks,* at the *Bedford-head?*" (*Sat.* II.ii.149–50); immoderation: "That both Extremes were banish'd from their walls,/ Carthusian Fasts and fulsome Bacchanals" (*Sat. Donne* II.117–18); imposition: "I puke, I nauseate,—yet he thrusts in more" (*Sat. Donne* IV.153).

The last is an unpleasant quotation reminiscent of the consummately disgusting lines from the *Epilogue to the Satires. Dialogue II*, concerning the Hogs of Westphaly, which always make their mark on a reader—no doubt because they are so repulsive in their own right; also, perhaps, because they have been presaged by lines in *The Second Satire of Dr. John Donne:*

> Wretched indeed! but far more wretched yet
> Is he who makes his meal on others wit:
> 'Tis chang'd no doubt from what it was before,
> His rank digestion makes it wit no more:
> Sense, past thro' him, no longer is the same,
> For food digested takes another name. (ll. 29–34)

and in the first dialogue of the *Epilogue:*

> . . . all the well-whipt Cream of Courtly Sense,
> That first was *H—vy's, F—'s* next, and then
> The *S—te's,* and then *H—vy's* once agen. (ll. 70–72)

Yet when one reflects on the general, prandial setting of these poems, the image—so definitely not table-talk—has more force than ever. In the final misanthropic, or at least severely despairing poems, the reader sees Pope, in most un-Horatian fashion, offending his guest. "*Fr.* This filthy Simile, this beastly Line,/ Quite turns my Stomach—*P.* So does Flatt'ry mine" (*Epil. Sat.* II.181–82). So often the ammunition of a satirist, excrement is a product of what sustains him.

The poet and his reader have moved a long way from the

Epistle to Arbuthnot, where, ensconced in the safety of his home, Pope had come to discover his strengths, the power and impregnability of his situation in and above the world. Even there, however, his welfare was threatened by a poetaster "Happy! to catch me, just at Dinner-time" (l. 14). Pope's response was patient, generous: to Gildon, "I wish'd the man a dinner, and sate still" (l. 152). He drank with Cibber (l. 373). But the chief of his enemies, how thoroughly they depart from Pope's hospitable, convivial standards: Atticus, the autocrat of his table at Button's; Bufo with his flatulent diet—"Fed with soft Dedication all day long" (l. 233)—and his circle of sycophants who

> flatter'd ev'ry day, and some days eat:
> Till grown more frugal in his riper days,
> He pay'd some Bards with Port, and some with Praise,
> To some a dry Rehearsal was assign'd,
> And others (harder still) he pay'd in kind.
> *Dryden* alone (what wonder?) came not nigh,
> *Dryden* alone escap'd this judging eye:
> But still the Great have kindness in reserve,
> He help'd to bury whom he help'd to starve.   (ll. 240–48)

and Sporus, the effete "Curd of Ass's milk," the spaniel mumbling the game he dares not bite, the "Flatt'rer at the Board," the source of the forbidden fruit (ll. 306, 314, 328, 330)—in short: unwholesome food (ass's milk was supposed to be drunk quite fresh[2]), a poor eater, a bad guest, a bad provider. Pope and his circle, of course, are the opposite of all these things in the imagery of the satires. His philosophy, in Milton's words, resembles "a perpetual feast of nectar'd sweets,/ Where no crude surfeit reigns," for he is the son of a father "Healthy by Temp'rance

---

[2] Marjorie Nicolson and G. S. Rousseau, *"This Long Disease, My Life": Alexander Pope and the Sciences* (Princeton, 1968), pp. 43–44. For Pope's tendency to eat and drink too much, see p. 55.

and by Exercise" (l. 401)—the salutary balance that Bethel will recommend at the beginning of his Sermon: "Go work, hunt, exercise! (he thus began)/ Then scorn a homely dinner, if you can" (*Sat.* ii.ii.11–12). Pope's dining room, in the satires, is an eighteenth-century clean, well-lighted place. As I shall argue in the next chapter and at the conclusion of this book, even the comprehensive darkness of the completed *Dunciad* cannot fully obscure it, the glow of the fusion Pope effected, most notably in these *Popean* imitations, between his art and his historical self and circumstances.

8. The Dunciad, in Four Books:
One Dim Ray of Light

The triumph of Dulness, daughter of Chaos, is nowhere more evident in the completed *Dunciad* than in its conglomeration of prolegomena, notes variorum, notes upon notes, the "Hypercritics of Aristarchus," his account of the hero, advertisement, letter to the publisher, testimonies of authors, and appendices, and more—a jungle of commentary in which the poem stands like a lost temple. The poem is the center, however, and the poet's vision, when both jungle and temple are taken into account, though a very dark vision, is not unrelievedly pessimistic; or so I mean to demonstrate here by attention to the character of the narrator and to the effect of the pedantic overgrowth upon the poem.

The fourth book, first published in 1742 and added in the edition of 1743 to the revised remainder of the work, stands off from or above Books I–III, first published in 1728, in part because Pope employs a new and different narrator. Who—what sort of person—describes the action of the first three books? It is difficult to say, for the voice seems that of an intelligence rather than a man: intelligence because only that faculty could produce

such deft verse, yet not human because he, or it, has no stake
in what he is describing, seems frivolous. His general technique
is encomium of what in the same breath he identifies as base:
the goddess Dulness is a "fair Ideot" (I.13). His subject by nature
despicable, he does not need to insist upon the fact by setting
himself against it, so sometimes writes as if a dunce himself,
in opinions if not in style. The only consistency in the voice
which addresses Swift, in a passage dating from the *Variorum*
edition of 1729—

> Whether thou chuse Cervantes' serious air,
> Or laugh and shake in Rab'lais' easy chair,
> Or praise the Court, or magnify Mankind,
> Or thy griev'd Country's copper chains unbind;
> From thy Bœotia tho' her Pow'r retires,
> Mourn not, my SWIFT, at ought our Realm acquires,
> Here pleas'd behold her mighty wings out-spread
> To hatch a new Saturnian age of Lead.   (I.21–28)

—is the consistency of capriciousness, for the irony in the notion
of Swift's praising the court cannot otherwise be coupled with
the directness of the statement in the following line; and the
Swift who unchained his country must be expected to mourn
the advent of a new leaden age. No, from the title onward, the
first three books are spoken so directly to predictable responses
that the narrator need establish no moral authority. To write
on dulness is to write against it. The speaker may say what he
likes, for or against duncery, duncically or shrewdly, without
danger of being misunderstood. Given this freedom, Pope adopts
the general role of Dulness' singer, as the first verse paragraph
of the first book makes plain, and his muses are the Smithfield
Muses. In sentiment, the most Popean lines in the entire first
three books come from the mouth of not the narrator but the

subterranean prophet Settle: "Hibernian Politics, O Swift! thy fate;/ and Pope's, ten years to comment and translate" (III.330–31).

But the fourth book, as the argument indicates, by reason of its grave subject demands a new invocation. "This," writes Scriblerus in a footnote to the first lines, "is an Invocation of much Piety. The Poet willing to approve himself a genuine Son, beginneth by shewing (what is ever agreeable to *Dulness*) his high respect for *Antiquity* and a *Great Family*, how dull, or dark soever: Next declareth his love for *Mystery* and *Obscurity;* and lastly his Impatience to be *re-united* to her." Or does he? These are the lines:

> Yet, yet a moment, one dim Ray of Light
> Indulge, dread Chaos, and eternal Night!
>   Of darkness visible so much be lent,
> As half to shew, half veil the deep Intent.
> Ye Pow'rs! whose Mysteries restor'd I sing,
> To whom Time bears me on his rapid wing,
> Suspend a while your Force inertly strong,
> Then take at once the Poet and the Song.

As usual, Scriblerus' comment is not entirely misleading. The narrator continues to "sing" the mysteries of Dulness, with the implication of praising them, and he asks to be taken. But he asks that the song be taken too. The main thrust of the passage, less invocation than supplication, is *against* the force of encroaching dulness, is in the interests of light, even if the ray of the first line quickly becomes mere "darkness visible," and the plea is spoken not to the muses, Smithfield or otherwise, but to the progenitors of Dulness. The Smithfield Muses have dropped out of the poem, while the old reputable muses now lie "in ten-fold bonds" (IV.35).

Yet at the end of the fourth book come the lines:

> Oh Muse! relate (for you can tell alone,
> Wits have short Memories, and Dunces none)
> Relate, who first, who last resign'd to rest;
> Whose heads she partly, whose completely blest;
> What Charms could Faction, what Ambition lull,
> The Venal quiet, and intrance the Dull;
> 'Til drown'd was Sense, and Shame, and Right, and Wrong—
> O sing, and hush the Nations with thy Song!
>   * * * * * *
> In vain, in vain,—the all-composing Hour
> Resistless falls: The Muse obeys the Pow'r.   (iv.619–28)

Which muse is she? Is she a Smithfield muse, an instrument whereby Dulness may reduce the nations to stupid sleep? She seems obedient, unresisting at the end. Or is she the muse of Homer and Virgil, set apart from the dunces by her capacity to remember, capable of hushing the cacophony of nonsense that has filled the four books, finally obedient to Dulness because, in such an age of overwhelming darkness, no other course remains. She seems at least as much the latter as the former—certainly in the poet's eyes, for he is asking her to do something resistant to Dulness. Perhaps she is best identified with one of the chained muses described earlier, still somehow capable of beneficent action: "There sunk Thalia, nerveless, cold, and dead./ Had not her sister Satyr held her head" (iv.41–42): the muse of satire. Sister of comedy, she has, until the last—perhaps beyond the last—held out the possibility of a happy ending. As Scriblerus notes, "She alone of all the sisters is unconquerable, never to be silenced, when truly inspired and animated (as should seem) from above, for this very purpose, to oppose the kingdom of Dulness to her last breath."

As for the narrator: There are signs alerting readers to possible

differences between the speaker of Books I–III and the speaker
of Book IV, for example a comment in the Advertisement to
The New Dunciad (1742): "That the author of the three first books
had a design to extend and complete his poem in this manner,
appears from the dissertation prefixt to it. . . . But whether or no
he be the author of this, we declare ourselves ignorant" (p. 411).
In the first note to this fourth book it is affirmed—by Scriblerus
in 1742, by Bentley in 1743—that the author is the same; Bentley
re- (or pre-) affirms it in a note to line 20 dating from 1742.
And these signs have significance, the narrator *is* different in the
fourth book because he no longer speaks as a celebrant of Dulness,
a voice he used intermittently through the earlier books, usually
characterized by quasi-oxymoronic phrases like "Curl's chaste
press" (I.40) and "the mighty Mad in Dennis" (I.106). Seldom
does he wax enthusiastic in similes like

> She saw, with joy, the line immortal run,
> Each sire imprest and glaring in his son:
> So watchful Bruin forms, with plastic care,
> Each growing lump, and brings it to a Bear   (I.101–4)

and seldom, as here with "lump" and "Bear," does he neatly,
superciliously topple an adulatory statement with a harsh *mot
juste* near the end—"Then raptures high the seat of Sense o'erflow./
Which only heads refin'd from Reason know" (III.5–6)—a device
like that whereby Dryden has Shadwell never deviate into *sense*.
Another, more elaborate *Mac Flecknoe*, the first three books of
The Dunciad describe folly comically, Dryden's poem being
comical because his dunces, despite the panoply of their procession, finally have control of only the realms of nonsense, in a
run-down back-corner of London. There is nothing threatening
about them, no goddess providing for them; power rests with
the witty, erudite poet who puts them through their tricks. In

just such a fashion, if at curiously unjoking length, does Pope describe the insignificant aberrations of his dunces until the end of Book III, which closes with Settle's prophecy wafting through the ivory gate of pipedreams.

Book IV is another story, the subject matter different, the times changed, the narrator fleshed out, *in* rather than above the action, a participant—and threatened. "Yes, the last Pen for freedom let me draw," as he said in the *Epilogue to the Satires*. The season for jokes is past. Instead of the mischievous wit who expatiated in ultimately ludicrous similes we hear a speaker contracted into small statements between quotations from Dulness and the dunces who are taking over the world. Instead of the amusing "sinking" in the action of the earlier books, especially the diving of the second, there is a true if ghastly sublime: the universal uncreation. (Longinus *had* famously cited the beginning of Genesis as an example of sublimity.) Instead of a playful, inconsistent narrator who seems sometimes himself an ally of the dunces, the speaker of Book IV will rise to Jeremian sternness:

> Now flam'd the Dog-star's unpropitious ray,
> Smote ev'ry Brain, and wither'd ev'ry Bay;
> Sick was the Sun, the Owl forsook his bow'r,
> The moon-struck Prophet felt the madding hour:
> Then rose the Seed of Chaos, and of Night,
> To blot out Order, and extinguish Light,
> Of dull and venal a new World to mold,
> And bring Saturnian days of Lead and Gold.   (IV.9–16)

Slightly revised, these lines would not look out of place in *Paradise Lost*, or the *Agamemnon* for that matter. The voice speaking them, far from reintroducing the banter of the address to Swift in Book I, speaks with directness and sympathy when reaching the equivalent passage of the final book: "Nor cou'd'st thou, CHESTERFIELD! a tear refuse,/ Thou wept'st, and with thee wept

each gentle Muse" (ɪᴠ.43–44). When the voice condemns, it does
so with resounding straightforwardness: "And (last and worst)
with all the cant of wit,/ Without the soul, the Muse's Hypocrit"
(ɪᴠ. 99–100). Historically, it is the voice of a poet who—unlike
the author of Books ɪ–ɪɪɪ—knows that readers now do recognize
who is the author of *The Dunciad;* in fact, know the author well
on the basis of the conversational, autobiographical, simulta-
neously private and public epistles and satires that he published
between the first three books and the fourth.[1] But I shall say
more about that topic in Part ɪɪɪ of this book.

Why does the poet bother to speak at all in the face of impending annihilation? Why compose a song that will quickly be
taken, with himself, by inexorably advancing primordial Chaos
and Night? Such imagery promises that apocalyptically, in the
manner of the Second Coming which is prophesied, Dulness
and her parents shall here recapitulate, inversely, the action of
those books of *Paradise Lost* wherein the Son forms the universe
from the stuff of chaos. All shall lose its form, not a rack behind.
But that is to overstate the case; although everything subsides
in sleep, not the world but simply the vigor of civilization shall
be destroyed, the vitality of the arts, religion, morality (to con-
dense the train of allegorical figures at the end). The dunces
shall live on, dormant as ever. Time shall take the poet and his
song—and the song shall be preserved. The train at the end of
Book ɪᴠ recalls that at the beginning, which I have mentioned
in speaking of the muse Pope addresses, the muse who reveals
some degree of activity though chained. And Satire is not the
only figure still herself, for

---

[1] Nearly two hundred lines of Book ɪᴠ, as Pope told Joseph Spence, were in
fact "first designed for an Epistle on Education, as part of my essay-scheme"
(ɪᴠ.149*n*), that is, Pope's Magnum Opus, the projected but uncompleted philosophical and poetical work that would have commenced with *An Essay on Man*
and would have included the *Moral Essays* and other, comparable epistles.

> There to her heart sad Tragedy addrest
> The dagger wont to pierce the Tyrant's breast;
> But sober History restrain'd her rage,
> And promis'd Vengeance on a barb'rous age.   (iv.37–40)

The joke and final consolation of *The Dunciad* are that the poem survives the apocalypse it describes, preserved by the dunces themselves, who have printed, edited, annotated, and garnished this account of them, this history, this satire.

The "scholarship" conspicuously encasing the poem from the 1729 *Variorum* on implies a fictional editing process that may be described as follows. An anonymous Advertisement, included in all subsequent editions and usually ascribed to the "publisher," bears the explanation: "The Commentary which attends the Poem, was sent me from several hands, and consequently must be unequally written" (p. 8). But the commentary itself would imply that Scriblerus, whether or not he has taken part in the final stage of preparation for the press, is the person most responsible for the editing: his are most of the signed notes and prolegomena, and he is given credit for his work on the title page. A nonce addendum, the "Errata" included in "The Second Edition" (the 1729*d* version), suggests that Scriblerus exercises continuing responsibility for supervision of publication. But some time before the appearance of the four-book *Dunciad* in 1743, chief editorship seems to have passed from Scriblerus to Richard Bentley, the putative author of "Ricardus Aristarchus of the Hero of the Poem"—an essay which is the main addition to the introductory material and which is designed to correct Scriblerus' commentary. Although most signed notes in the 1743 *Dunciad* still bear the name Scriblerus, Bentley's primacy in editorial responsibility seems clear because of a note, by Scriblerus, to the passage in Book iv that describes Bentley: "The Compliment paid by our author to this eminent Professor, in applying to him so great a Name, was the reason that he hath omitted to comment on this part which contains his own praises. We shall therefore supply that loss to our best ability" (IV.210n). This is the only occasion in all the apparatus of *The Dunciad* when Scriblerus writes as if aware of Bentley's notes, whereas in several places Bentley comments upon the notes of Scriblerus, usually to disagree. For example, in the three-book *Dunciad*, Scriblerus has signed this gloss on the opening lines of Book III: "Hereby is intimated that the following Vision is no more than the Chimera of the Dreamer's brain, and not a real or intended satire on the Present Age, doubtless more learned, more inlighten'd, and more abounding with great Genius's in Divinity, Politics, and whatever Arts and Sciences, than all the preceding. For fear of any such mistake of our Poet's honest meaning, he hath again at the end of this Vision, repeated this monition, saying that it all past thro' the *Ivory gate*, which (according to the Ancients) denoteth Falsity." In the 1743 version, Bentley adds: "How much the good Scriblerus was mistaken, may be seen from the Fourth book, which, it is plain from hence, he had never seen." But Scriblerus has written and signed footnotes to the fourth book as reprinted here! What is more, though seemingly compelled to disagree with Scriblerus' interpretation of the ivory gate at the beginning of the book, Bentley does not contradict the same point as repeated by Scriblerus in the note to III.333. The vigilance of the general editor lapses.

Thus, to summarize a bewildering matter, in the three-book version, from 1729 on, an anonymous publisher has put in final form the apparatus contributed by a number of hands, predominantly by Scriblerus, who also serves as chief editor of the fourth book when it appears for the first time, by itself, in 1742. In 1743, with the publication of *The Dunciad, in Four*

Books, Bentley has succeeded Scriblerus as general editor; as I have said, the initial note to Book iv is signed Scriblerus in 1742, Bentley in 1743. Yet also in 1743 Scriblerus has entered like an emeritus editor to supply what Bentley is too modest to perform, notes upon Aristarchus-Bentley. The matter does become confusing, especially because forebearant Scriblerus emeritus has let stand some notes in which Bentley contradicts him, one such note depending from the earliest lines of the fourth book: when the narrator asks for visible darkness "half to shew, half veil the deep Intent" of Dulness (iv.4), Scriblerus—still regarding the poet as an ally of the goddess—comments, "This is a great propriety, for a dull Poet can never express himself otherwise than by *halves,* or imperfectly"; Bentley adds, "I understand it very differently; the Author in this work had indeed a *deep Intent;* there were in it Mysteries . . . which he durst not fully reveal." Perhaps this is merely deference, on the part of joint-editors, to each other's opinion—or, since Bentley had died in 1742, perhaps Scriblerus has been recalled to complete, respectfully, his successor's task. Enough. The fiction of the editing process cannot be discerned fully, itself another example of what the poem ridicules. Moreover, the fiction leads imperceptibly into life and the notes contributed by Pope's officious, erudite, but ostentatious friend William Warburton.[2]

If only to exercise dulness upon it, the dunces will preserve

[2] The "Advertisement to the Reader" (1743), signed W. W., would suggest that Warburton was general editor of *The Dunciad, in Four Books,* but he initialed no notes until the edition of 1751. Hence, apart from the Advertisement, in 1743 the work of editing is mainly attributable to Scriblerus and Bentley. The myth of editing had secondary advantages: when Aaron Hill complained of a note abusing him, Pope replied, "Would you have the Note *left out?* It shall. Would you have it expressly said, *you were not meant?* It shall, if I have any influence on the Editors" (*Correspondence,* ed. George Sherburn [5 vols.; Oxford, 1956], iii, 171).

their epic. Had they wanted to destroy it, they would probably not have succeeded, since "it is the common effect of Dulness (even in her greatest efforts) to defeat her own design" (IV. 584*n*). In fact, they have—according to Pope's fiction—preserved *The Dunciad*. The very presentation of the poem in an elaborate frame of scholarship suggests that it is a classic work of some antiquity, an impression the commentators reinforce from time to time. Writes Scriblerus in the essay "Of the Poem": "We shall next declare the occasion and the cause which moved our Poet to this particular work. He lived in those days, when (after providence had permitted the Invention of Printing as a scourge for the Sins of the learned) Paper also became so cheap, and printers so numerous, that a deluge of authors cover'd the land" (p. 49). The Advertisement to the first edition of Book IV, and Bentley's initial note, indicate that the author is unknown; while the supposedly unattributable fourth book, *The New Dunciad: As it was Found in the Year 1741,* "was found," according to the Advertisement, "merely by accident, in taking a survey of the *Library* of a late eminent nobleman; but in so blotted a condition, and in so many detach'd pieces, as plainly shewed it to be not only *incorrect,* but *unfinished"* (pp. 410–11), and evidently extant for some time. How long is hinted in an anonymous note late in the book, added in 1743: "These Verses were written many years ago, and may be found in the State Poems of that time. So that Scriblerus is mistaken or whoever else have imagined this Poem of a fresher date" (IV.615*n*). The parodic proclamation, also attached in 1743, indicates that the Lord Chancellor, not the author, has "revised" the poem to make Cibber the hero, replacing Theobald (p. 252).

The new narrator of the 1743 *Dunciad* is gone, the poem survives. Scriblerus, Bentley, *et al.*—his critics and commentators—proliferate. Dulness' empire is restored. But after all, restoration was conceivable only because she had once before been conquered; she may be conquered again. History and satire, immortal, live on in the text the dunces themselves preserve, a text to which the curious and sometimes contradictory, often duncical notes inevitably conduct the reader. Life is short, art enduring; a better time may come, and with it an audience that merits the poem. To quote the peroration of Ricardus Aristarchus, though not to the purpose he intended: "Nothing therefore (we conceive) remains to hinder his own Prophecy of himself from taking immediate effect. A rare felicity! and what few prophets have had the satisfaction to see, alive! Nor can we conclude better than with that extraordinary one of his, which is conceived in these Oraculous words, MY DULNESS WILL FIND SOMEBODY TO DO IT RIGHT."

Part 2. Acts

9. Transitions

During ten years out of the middle of his writing life, the years between 1718 and 1727, Pope published almost no original poems of importance, an interval concluded by the first version of *The Dunciad*—a poem spoken in a voice unlike any he had used before. In the course of this brief portrait of the poet I shall try to account for that change and for his selection of the voices one hears in the later works, especially the Horatian epistles and the final *Dunciad*. My subject is Pope, the poet and the man; my purpose, as much as possible to draw the poet and the man together.[1]

If one had to choose a single word to describe the person who speaks to us in the earlier public poems, those published before the 1720s, before the translation of Homer was completed, and meant (unlike certain of his anonymous *jeux d'esprit*) to be associated permanently with his name, one might do worse than choose

---

[1] Throughout this part I have depended so heavily upon George Sherburn's *The Early Career of Alexander Pope*, (Oxford, 1934) that exhaustive documentation would be cumbersome. I therefore confine my references to matters of weight. References in the text to Pope's *Correspondence*, ed. Sherburn (5 vols.; Oxford, 1956) are distinguishable by their volume numbers from references to the biography.

the word "diffident." The poet of the *Pastorals* and *Messiah,* the
Essay on Criticism, Windsor-Forest, and *The Rape of the Lock* is a
model young man, gifted but unfailingly humble: the modest
thrush of *Spring,* the "Candidate for Praise" who concludes *The
Temple of Fame* by praying, "Unblemish'd let me live, or die unknown," the peaceful, retired denizen of *Windsor-Forest,* the playful yet sensible narrator who so courteously reminds Belinda of
her mortality. Here is a winning youth whom any reputable older
man would be quick to adopt—filial as Aeneas, capable of occasional acerbities but in general a marvel of soft modulation.
His Anchises? There were several: besides his actual father, he
had Sir William Trumbull and "Knowing," fashionable William
Walsh, who draped the mantle of correctness about his shoulders.
Years later, in the *Epistle to Dr. Arbuthnot,* Pope would recall his
being encouraged by fine older men (ll. 135–46). But he did not
delay in showing gratitude. He was all gratitude; as early as *An
Essay on Criticism,* his first conversational poem (1711), he is a man
speaking to men yet a young man, who, when he speaks of himself, almost vanishes in the glow of his sense of obligation to
Walsh:

> This Praise at least a grateful Muse may give!
> The Muse, whose early Voice you taught to Sing,
> Prescrib'd her Heights, and prun'd her tender Wing,
> (Her Guide now lost) no more attempts to *rise,*
> But in low Numbers short Excursions tries:
> Content, if hence th' Unlearn'd their Wants may view,
> The Learn'd reflect on what before they knew:
> Careless of *Censure,* nor too fond of *Fame,*
> Still pleas'd to praise, yet not afraid to blame,
> Averse alike to *Flatter,* or *Offend,*
> Not *free* from Faults, nor yet too vain to mend.   (ll. 734–44)

Yet in and alongside proclamations of his humility he does keep
talking about himself, to the extent that the subject becomes

almost conventional at the close of each larger poem. Besides the examples I have given, there are the indulgent self-deprecation of the *Epistle to Mr. Jervas,* "Thou but preserv'st a Face and I a Name," and the melancholy lines on the poet that conclude the *Elegy to the Memory of an Unfortunate Lady.* As if by habit he even makes Eloisa advert to him when finishing her monologue!

In these three later poems, published during 1716–17, the voice mixes humility with more sadness than youthful enthusiasm, and whereas the poems of 1709–14 promoted public virtue as well as private—judgment, piety, good sense, justice and peace, in *An Essay on Criticism, Messiah, The Rape of the Lock, Windsor-Forest*—the poems of 1715–17 have more to do with private experience, stressing, in a not unsentimental manner, the mutability and pain inseparable from fame, art, and love. But whether personal, social, political, or theological the poet's values tend to be absolute: he speaks of a grace beyond the reach of art, a peace surpassing that attained at Utrecht, a degree of good sense Belinda will not achieve, a love Eloisa cherishes in impossible circumstances. And accordingly, the poems tend to be ceremonial, presenting settings and actions at a definite remove from ordinary experience. Shepherds sing, the Messiah comes and trees dance upon mountains, Father Thames speaks forth, a lock of hair soars into the sky, a poet has allegorical visions of Fame and Rumor's temples, a nun raves, the ghost of a dead lady appears. Time tends not to pass, either interrupted by some great event— parousia, theophany, apotheosis, ecstasy, apparition—or fixed in recurrent cycles, like the seasons of the *Pastorals* and *Windsor-Forest.* The poet sits outside the action, contemplative and serviceable, and above all unimpeachable, an aspiring *vates* of the old verities: Virtue, Honor, Truth and Candor, Justice, the Duties of the Wise and Good, and the rest of those stately words that lift their capitals throughout the poems.

"'Tis no flattery at all to say, that *Virgil* had written nothing so good at his age" (1.7) wrote Walsh to William Wycherley in 1705, referring to the *Pastorals*. Somewhat breathlessly, George Granville wrote to a friend about this "young Poet, newly inspir'd . . .; his name is *Pope;* he is not above Seventeen or Eighteen Years of Age, and promises Miracles: if he goes on as he has begun, in the Pastoral way, as *Virgil* first try'd his Strength, we may hope to see *English* Poetry vie with the Roman, and this Swan of Windsor sing as sweetly as the *Mantuan*" (p. 52). Such a comparison was inevitable, was doubtless courted by the youth who begàn his poetical novitiate in the canonical manner. Like Virgil he begins with pastorals, then in *Windsor-Forest* attempts something not unlike the *Georgics,* a poem of rural life with heroic overtones, natural description civilized. Like someone bringing a lute up to pitch, he slowly ascends the scale of the heroic, from *Windsor-Forest* to the mock majesty of the perfected *Rape of the Lock,* finally to the small but unquestionably high form of heroic epistle in *Eloisa to Abelard*. Then what better preparation for a great English poem (he had earlier written a short epic on "Alcander," perhaps Aeneas' companion of that name, and later would meditate an epic on Brutus, the legendary Aeneas of England)—what better preparation than translating all Homer? Then ten years of editing and translation, followed by *The Dunciad,* ten years of virtual silence culminating in a negative *Aeneid* describing the progress of dulness, written by a narrator who, as I have argued, is indistinguishable in his stated principles from the dunces he lampoons. In effect, the silence is prolonged here, as well as in the voice of Martinus Scriblerus, Pope's foolish spokesman of the *Peri Bathous* (1728) and *Dunciad Variorum* (1729). Moreover, the silence may be said to commence not after, but in, *Eloisa to Abelard*—especially if my questions about its orthodoxy are thought tenable, but even if they are not, for while *Eloisa* is Pope's first thoroughly heroic poem on a human theme (as distinguished from the divine theme of *Messiah*), it is also his first important poem not written *in propria persona*. Eloisa speaks of the poet, he nowhere speaks of himself. For years, from this point, the promising young poet will be in eclipse and the Virgilian possibilities will fade. When, in *The Dunciad*, the shade of Elkanah Settle prophesies in accents more like Pope's than those of anything the narrator says, the speech has a post-lapsarian ring: "Hibernian Politicks, O Swift, thy doom,/ And Pope's, translating three whole years with Broome" (III.327–28). As if William Broome had employed Pope and not the reverse, but I shall say more of this later.

Return Alpheus: with the 1730s, the poet again discovers a voice, in *An Essay on Man* a voice resembling that of the old—young—Pope, who seems to find in Bolingbroke a Walsh for his middle age:

> Come then, my Friend, my Genius, come along,
> Oh master of the poet, and the song!
> And while the Muse now stoops, or now ascends,
> To Man's low passions, or their glorious ends,
> Teach me, like thee, in various nature wise,
> To fall with dignity, with temper rise;
> Form'd by thy converse, happily to steer
> From grave to gay, from lively to severe;
> Correct with spirit, eloquent with ease,
> Intent to reason, or polite to please.
> Oh! while along the stream of Time thy name
> Expanded flies, and gathers all its fame,
> Say, shall my little bark attendant sail,
> Pursue the triumph, and partake the gale? (IV.373–86)

The speaker of at least this passage of *An Essay on Man* spoke also at the conclusion of *An Essay on Criticism*. The later essay has also, like the earlier poems, a set of doctrines more *a priori* than otherwise, and it represents a world in which Nature can enjoy a theophany, a relatively timeless world wherein history but repeats the obvious or at least the general and abstract and absolute: either one confesses that "Wisdom infinite must form the best" or one does not. As Bolingbroke's vicar, Pope asserts all the authority he can draw from the traditions and tone at his disposal. But apart from *An Essay on Man*, in the *Moral Essays* and the *Imitations of Horace* — that is, in the bulk of his poetry of the thirties — Pope writes differently, much differently, and the world he represents is more recognizable than that of the early poems, the sense of time different, and the standards, and the self of the poet. Personifications and fancied characters do not speak; the poet and his friends and enemies do. The world is the quotidian world, the design of the poems conversational. The standards are rooted in experience, more relative, more complicated, living, lived by a man in, not above, the life he writes about, a man among men. The new Pope has more than one way of speaking to a Bolingbroke:

> You laugh, half Beau half Sloven if I stand,
> My Wig all powder, and all snuff my Band;
> You laugh, if Coat and Breeches strangely vary,
> White Gloves, and Linnen worthy Lady Mary!
> But when no Prelate's Lawn with Hair-shirt lin'd,
> Is half so incoherent as my Mind,
> When (each Opinion with the next at strife,
> One ebb and flow of follies all my Life)
> I plant, root up, I build, and then confound,
> Turn round to square, and square again to round;
> You never change one muscle of your face,
> You think this Madness but a common case,
> Nor once to Chanc'ry, nor to Hales apply;
> Yet hang your lip, to see a Seam awry!
> Careless how ill I with myself agree;
> Kind to my dress, my figure, not to Me.
> Is this my Guide, Philosopher, and Friend?

> This, He who loves me, and who ought to mend?
> Who ought to make me (what he can, or none,)
> That Man divine whom Wisdom calls her own,
> Great without Title, without Fortune bless'd,
> Rich ev'n when plunder'd, honour'd while oppress'd,
> Lov'd without youth, and follow'd without power,
> At home tho' exil'd, free, tho' in the Tower.
> In short, that reas'ning, high, immortal Thing,
> Just less than Jove, and much above a King,
> Nay half in Heav'n—except (what's mighty odd)
> A fit of Vapours clouds this Demi-god.

The passages, from *An Essay on Man* and from the conclusion of *The First Epistle of the First Book of Horace Imitated*, respectively, are companion pieces. In them Pope shows himself to be "in various nature wise," able himself "happily to steer/ From grave to gay, from lively to severe," as he would have Bolingbroke teach him—and be. The poet who in the early works would come on at the end for a decorous bow, now has become performer as well as author and, it need not be argued, an attractive subject. Even in *An Essay on Man*, as I have asserted, the speaker stands closer to the reader than does the Great Chain of Being.

What I have said so briefly raises several questions, particularly: did not the forms Pope chose, for example the Horatian epistle, determine the kind of voice one hears in the poems? Do I not suggest too positive a view of Pope's final self, neglecting as I have the despondent *Epilogue to the Satires* (1738) and the final, four-book *Dunciad* (1742–43)? To the first question I shall answer only that Pope did choose the forms. To the second, more significant question, I shall reply in the chapter that concludes this part of my essay.

10. Toyshop and Boneshop

The poet is a veritable Galahad in the important early poems, then, after ten years' silence, writes at length with a show of insouciance on the subject of dulness' triumph. If the narrator of *The Dunciad* of 1728 has any character at all, it is the character of a hack like those he celebrates. His muses are the Smithfield Muses. Is it possible that this change in the poet's character has more than rhetorical significance, that the narrator of *The Dunciad* differs from the narrator of the early poems because Pope's personality had changed? So guarded was he about his innermost life, even in letters to friends, that the question cannot be answered definitively, but speculation on the topic may nevertheless have some interest, especially to those who think the chief significance of his life derives from his works. If all the poems may be said to constitute one long work, it is worthwhile to attempt accounting for the discontinuities.

Pope's defensiveness may be the most conspicuous trait in an elusive personality. Not that his personality was elusive in every respect: most of the time he worked hard to portray himself, in his poems and letters, as a modest man who, despite disadvantages physical and social, strenuously upheld the virtue of charity, to parents, friends, everyone; compared to this, he would protest, his poetry was insignificant: authors like himself "write only for the present Ear, & are (as St. Paul expresses it) only as a Tinkling Cymbal" (II. 472). And not that he lacked good social and physical reasons for defensiveness: four-foot-six in his prime, hunchbacked, chronically ill; a papist (named Pope!) in a nation itself defensive about its Protestantism since it had driven out James II, during the year of the poet's birth; debarred from the universities, the government, and some professions; subjected to extra taxation; suspected of sympathy for the Roman Catholic pretenders to the crown; harassed by picayune legislation, for example the laws against living in London or buying real estate. Brought up in the country, largely self-educated, when in his later teens he made his way into London life, he came encrusted with rusticity. He had every reason to be self-conscious, and he early discovered a mode of self-description that afforded protection against most eventualities. He lost no time before first emitting that note of retirement's consolations which reverberates through poems early and late, in the *Ode on Solitude:* "Happy the man, whose wish and care/ A few paternal acres bound," happy because blest with food, clothing, shade, shelter, health, peace,

>   . . . study and ease
>   Together mix'd; sweet recreation,
>   And innocence, which most does please,
>   With Meditation.
>
>   Thus let me live, unseen, unknown;
>   Thus unlamented let me dye;
>   Steal from the world, and not a stone
>   Tell where I lye.

When he wrote this in its first version he was just twelve years old.

His standards were high, his expectations minimal. Precocious person that he was, he remained only briefly a boy but took a long time to become an adult. The older men, that trio of Williams — Trumbull, Walsh, Wycherley — early drew him away from the things of youth, yet kept him in a filial position with patronage of their "little" Pope. Sherburn remarks that as a boy the poet seems to have had few companions his own age.[1] Soon unfit for vigorous activity in any case, he was admonished to be correct, not just by Walsh but earlier by his careful father, who encouraged him to write verses and sent him back to revise them until they were perfect. In their Catholic, country home, Pope's retired father, who would later frown upon some of his son's London acquaintances (p. 62), cultivated piety and letters as well as his garden.

Yet the talented youth wished to see what he might do — encouraged as he was, who would not? Extremely alert, he quickly discerned the feelings of others and found that he had a genius for responding to their expectations. He is a chameleon in his letters, something to everybody but by himself almost undefinable: a critic with Walsh, a wit with Wycherley, a rake with Henry Cromwell (his friend in London), a pious Catholic with John Caryll (his country correligionist); "So," Pope wrote to Cromwell in 1710 after enduring Lent in the Forest, "just as I am drunk or Scandalous in Town, according to my Company, I am for the same reason Grave & Godly here" (1.81). The personality revealed in his earlier letters seems less elusive than protean, and with the success of his *Pastorals*, published in 1709 but circulated before that among connoisseurs, he became eager to see whether he might succeed in London despite his disabilities. The *Essay on Criticism* (1711) is particularly interesting as a bid for attention and acclaim by a politically suspect ·young papist.

---

[1] "With fox-hunting youths of his own age he had little in common," Sherburn adds in "Pope on the Threshold of His Career," *Harvard Library Bulletin*, XIII (1959), 32.

Just as later he would try to laugh feuding families together by means of *The Rape of the Lock*, in the *Essay* — an *ars poetica laici* — he disparages the factionalism of politics and minimizes differences in religion, so much so that he offended his Roman Catholic friends. The tactic worked well: though as a papist he would be thought an ally of the Tories, he saw his poem praised in the Whig *Spectator*, which the next year printed his *Messiah*. Above parties and sects, conspicuously talented and thus potentially dangerous if alienated, he was courted by men of all sides and proved reasonably accommodating in all directions. In 1713, though becoming intimate with his Tory Scriblerus associates, he wrote for Steele's *Guardian* and composed the prologue to Addison's *Cato*. In his delicate manner he even ventured to propagandize for the Tory Peace of Utrecht, in *Windsor-Forest* — carefully enough that readers of both parties might find something to agree with. He bestrode London, briefly; then the death of Queen Anne in 1714 opened so wide a chasm that continued success became impossible. Although he had avoided factional entanglements, friendship demands more than high-mindedness, and his better friends were Tories. The moodiness of the poems published between 1715 and 1717 may reflect his disappointment.

Meanwhile he felt he needed money, incongruous as that need seemed with his vocation—as he regarded it—and his acquired social position. In a letter to Caryll he had politely regretted "suffering any consideration so dirty as that of money to have place in a letter of friendship" (I.155). "*Let not such things*, as the apostle saith," he later, brazenly, wrote to William Broome, his collaborator, on the *Odyssey*, "*be so much as named amongst ye*" (II.397). But he was not a gentleman, though he occasionally pretended to be. He was the son of a retired merchant, dependent on a small income sometimes threatened by the hazards of the market. He was not employed. When his father died, in 1717, Pope would write in a letter: "He has left me to the ticklish Management of a narrow Fortune, where every false Step is dangerous" (i.455). So he began to translate the *Iliad* to make his own fortune, a project that soon grew forbidding and tedious, before that embroiling him in controversy over the rival translation begun by Thomas Tickell and supported by Addison. He complains frequently in his letters about physical and emotional strains.

It is customary for critics and biographers to minimize, even ridicule, Pope's ardent letters to Lady Mary Wortley Montagu, and Sherburn rather abruptly dismisses the question of Pope's relations with Martha Blount: "Whether she was Pope's mistress is now nobody's business: no evidence of the slightest validity, apart from the unusualness of their friendship, has ever been adduced to indicate such a relationship" (p. 291).[2] But it may be that Pope's later bitterness about Lady Mary is explicable only as the consequence of rejection, and those elegiac poems—Eloisa's and that of the "Unfortunate Lady"—certainly, as Sherburn says, express pathos, the suffering of a man whom John Dennis had once stigmatized, in print, as "the very bow of the God of Love" (p. 92). Pope could turn upon the Blount sisters as severely as he did upon Lady Mary: witness the letter in which, temporarily breaking with them, he cries, "I have heard indeed of Women that have had a kindness for Men of my Make; but it has been after Enjoyment, never before" (i.456). What did Pope see when he snuffed out the light? He was not one to say, but toward the close of the second decade of the century, when he was approach-

---

[2] F. W. Bateson brings together what evidence there is, arguing that such a relationship was "not improbable," in the Introduction to *Epistles to Several Persons (Moral Essays)*, Vol. iii-ii of the Twickenham Edition (2d ed.; London, 1961), p. 47n. Scandalous rumors gnawed at Pope during the critical time after the *Odyssey* had begun to be published, according to a letter to Caryll (ii.353).

ing thirty and his early patrons had all slipped from him, his
thoughts must have run on money and women. He mentions
nightmares about translating the *Iliad* (pp. 186–187), and in a
fey letter of 1718 to the Blount sisters he fantasizes about the
Day of Judgment, when "those white Bums which I dye to see,
will be shown to all the world" (1.515). His mind ranged well
beyond the contentment of a few acres, though when his father
died and the house at Twickenham was leased, he threw much
energy into their improvement, and his headaches were not all
somatic. Frustrated as he seems to have been in love, he would
not be—could not afford to be—defeated in business, as his letters
show, filled as they are with minute attention to the details of
winning and satisfying subscribers to the *Iliad*, later the *Odyssey*
and the edition of Shakespeare. One particularly enterprising
friend had the satisfaction of seeing her name in the subscribers'
list of the *Odyssey* printed in capitals, with a star, as a premium
for gathering so many subscriptions.

The years of translating and editing were vexed in several
ways: besides the matters I have mentioned, there was the trial
of Bishop Atterbury, Pope's close friend prosecuted for treason
as a consequence of involvement in a Jacobite plot, and the tem-
porary suppression of the Jacobitical *Works* of the Duke of Buckingham, which Pope had edited. Both events of 1723 were dangerous to the welfare, not to mention the projects, of a Catholic
poet. But worse was to come. Despite the troubles he had endured
for years—the life of a wit, he remarked, echoing Job, is a warfare
on the earth—he could always retreat to that attitude of the solitary contemplative, immure himself in his grotto with "innocence, which most does please." Utterly jealous of his reputation,
so much so that one may suppose he found his identity excessively
in others' eyes, he had always managed, even after he had entered

the marketplace in earnest, to make sure that—whatever men
might say, the Curlls of this world—no one would *prove* him
anything but the paragon he says he is in his poems. If one takes
that attitude seriously, one will recognize that the circumstances
surrounding the publication of Pope's *Odyssey* in 1725–26 must
have been grievous for the poet to endure. It may be argued not
only that this, as Maynard Mack says, was "the most disreputable
episode in a career not free of disreputable episodes,"[3] but also
that the difficulties of this time, this event just preceding his
work on *The Dunciad*, affected Pope more deeply than anything
in his life thus far.

Secretly, he had employed Elijah Fenton and William Broome
to translate certain books of the *Odyssey*, though, in his proposals,
seeming to promise that the performance would, like the translation of the *Iliad*, be entirely his own. Financial considerations
were as important as any in the formation of this scheme: a man
could employ collaborators, but to the extent that the collaborators were less distinguished than he, the profits would be less,
subscriptions more difficult to gain. Then, before publication,
Broome let it be known that he had helped Pope, and immediately there was a furor among those enemies Pope had always
been able to hold at bay. As never before, the poet was compromised—and seemingly reacted in panic. He would not outrightly
admit the fact of collaboration, he could not deny it, so he finally
minimized it. He added to the notes at the end a statement signed
by Broome to the effect that Pope's helpers were responsible for
only five of the twenty-four books, whereas in truth they had
done twelve (p. 260). Whatever the case, Pope was caught, publicly a deceiver. If a hack is one who writes for money and de-

---

[3] Introduction, *The Iliad of Homer*, ed. Maynard Mack, Vol. vii of the Twickenham Edition (London, 1967), p. xliv.

frauds readers by supplying something less than what he offers, Pope, for the first time in his life, seemed to be a hack.[4]

Sherburn comments, "One seems to note in his letters that the deeper he gets into the mire about the *Odyssey*, the more he protests the tenderness of his honour and honesty" (p. 291). To Broome he complains, in November of 1725, "I have been as sick of the translation as you can be of the notes, and indeed, as you know, have had many things to make me quite sour about it. I know myself to be an honest man, and, I will add, a friendly one; nor do I in my conscience think I have acted an unfair or disreputable part with the public, if my friends will do me justice" (II.339). In a Christmas letter he tells Caryll about the *Odyssey's* public reception, then insists: "I wish I had nothing to trouble me more: an honest mind is not in the power of any dishonest one. To break its peace, there must be some guilt or consciousness, which is inconsistent with its own principles" (II.353). He seems to have experienced more guilt than consciousness. Most revealingly, he had written about a month earlier to the same correspondent: "I believe not only the future but the present age will soon allow it to be an exacter version than that of the *Iliad* where all the drudgery was my own. When I translate again I will be hanged; nay I will do something to deserve to be hanged, which is worse, rather than drudge for such a world as is no judge

[4] As his enemies continually pointed out thereafter, beginning in late 1725 with remarks about "that late Jobb of Journey-Work, the Translation of Homer's ODYSSEY," about Pope's scheme to sell "a Book in his *own* Name by Subscription, and get a great part of it done by *Assistants*," about "Mr. *Pope's* patching up a Translation from different Hands, which he himself had promis'd," etc., etc.; see J. V. Guerinot, *Pamphlet Attacks on Alexander Pope, 1711–1744: A Descriptive Bibliography* (New York, 1969), pp. 94, 120, 130, and *passim.* Praising Pope's patience, Guerinot says, "He never, it might be pointed out, replied to any of the attacks on the *Iliad* and *Odyssey*, despite their number and vexatiousness" (p. 1). Pope's not replying, however, may illustrate discretion rather than forbearance.

of your labour. I'll sooner write something to anger it, than to please it" (II.341). His false advertising, his mercenary purpose—he mentions neither. Instead he represents himself as one who strove through collaboration to excel his singlehanded translation of the *Iliad*, and as one who wrote, who drudged, to benefit the world. The world is undiscriminating, ungrateful; as he had written to Broome a year before, "The public is both an unfair and a silly judge, unless it be led or trepanned into justice" (II.271); he will punish it. Yet he believes the same world will soon vindicate him. In his embarrassment and anger, unable to see himself, the work, and the public for what they are, he declares, in effect, Evil be thou my good. Accused of misconduct, he will respond with mischief; angry above all with himself, he blames everyone else. Interesting to note, only a month or so before telling Broome he would anger the world rather than please it, Pope had received that letter (ubiquitous in criticism of *Gulliver's Travels*) in which Swift pledges, "the chief end I propose to my self in all my labors is to vex the world rather than divert it" (II.325).

The shock of exposure must have been devastating. Throughout his works Pope had represented himself as a paragon of goodness, probity, public spirit, and there is no reason to think he did not privately regard himself as such. In adversity he had found self-esteem more durable than popularity. Though often assaulted, he walked safe behind a shield of righteousness somehow made compatible with strong poetic, social, and financial ambitions. In his self-regard there was, inevitably, a measure of Spartan hypocrisy, the crime above all not committing a crime but being caught. The attitude is easily associated with Pope's pains to publicize a spotless image of himself in his poems and letters, feeling as he did that (he says so in a letter to Broome just after the fact of collaboration became public) the world "will be ready, and for the majority, glad to take any opportunity to blame a man it has too long praised or, at least, been forced not to dispraise" (II.273). A boy growing up in the rays of a retired father and elderly retired friends, who maintain high standards of behavior more easily because of their withdrawal from the world with reputation intact, will probably find some of his own behavior better concealed than explained; a man belonging to a harried religious minority will be wary, whether or not he is a fervent member of the sect. That Pope harbored these feelings becomes evident long before the incident of the *Odyssey*. When enemies in 1716 printed his burlesque of the first psalm—Sherburn calls the poem a "tavern piece of truly impious buffoonery" —Pope placed in the newspapers a repudiation of the poem that, by his own admission in a letter to Martha Blount, was a neat example of equivocation (p. 181). A good man is jealous of his reputation, but so is a shrewd merchant or a winning youth. Pope tried to be all these things—until the affair of the *Odyssey* made the role of public saint impossible to sustain any longer. And the next year Lewis Theobald published *Shakespeare Restored* (1726), convicting Shakespeare's editor of blatant carelessness. That the voice Pope adopts in *The Dunciad* and the *Peri Bathous* is predominantly the voice of a hack, a laureate of Dulness and an encomiast of her works, and that, especially in the text of the poem, his personal bitterness is so unmistakable, have a psychological coherence with his experience of recent years that, while unprovable, should not be taken lightly. The voice of the three-book *Dunciad* is a voice desperately playful in perverse atonement for the most damaging kind of embarrassment. Pope's hatred for the dunces is perhaps best explained if one sees in it an expression of hatred for something in himself which cir-

cumstances have made so public that he cannot avoid recognizing it.[5] Regrettably he tries to make Broome the scapegoat, ridiculing him in *Peri Bathous* and *The Dunciad.*

The Dunciad, modeled on the *Aeneid,* about the triumph of not
Brutus but barbarism, turns out to be Pope's epic. Moreover,
The Dunciad is his last poem in the early style: heroic like *The
Rape of the Lock,* with the speaking ghost of Settle entering in
Book III to prophesy as Father Thames does in *Windsor-Forest,*
an apocalyptic prophecy that ultimately inverts the final vision
of *Messiah:* instead of "God's eternal Day," "universal Darkness."
The devices of heightening that formerly served his idealism now
express the depth of his hatred. Positive has become negative.
One may speculate about just how much Swift had to do with
this inversion—how much Swift possessed Pope to write as he
did. In the years just preceding the publication of *The Dunciad*
Swift paid his two last visits to England and Pope. Throughout
letters of the period Swift presses the poet to give the world "one
lash the more at my Request" (II.325). He tells Gay he hopes

---

[5] In the most authoritative study of eighteenth-century duncehood yet produced,
Pat Rogers suggests a darkened background for this scene of recognition, quoting
a letter Pope wrote in 1722—"I have wholly given over scribbling, at least any
thing of my own, but am become, by due gradation of dulness, from a poet a translator, and from a translator, a mere editor"—and commenting: "The tone is
amused and mock-regretful. But there is a serious element underlying it all: Pope's
genuine sorrow, and guilt, on realising that the best years of his life have been
given over to secondary pursuits, whether the version of Homer or the edition of
Buckinghamshire. His real mission in life has not been accomplished; his highest
literary appetencies have not been satisfied. Tomorrow he must go off and write
Essays on Man. This serious application is focused in the phrase 'due gradations
of dulness'. There *was* a duncely career, a typical life-cycle embracing high initial
aspirations, gradual disenchantment, acquiescence first in the mediocre and then
in the downright venal. [John] Oldmixon embodies, in his own biography, the
stages of such a descent into Dulness. His progressive tropism away from creative
writing and towards compilation exemplifies the 'due gradations' which Pope
observes" (*Grub Street: Studies in a Subculture* [London, 1972], p. 195).

"to see Popes Dullness knock down the Beggers Opera" (II.484). To Pope he writes: "You talk of this Dunciad, but I am impatient to have it *volare per ora*" (II.492–93). He gives advice about the preparation of the next edition (II.504–5). Surely there was nothing gratuitous about Pope's dedicating the poem to the author of *Gulliver* and of, particularly, *A Tale of a Tub;* "Certainly without you it had never been," Pope wrote to him (II.522), and the poet told Thomas Sheridan that Swift was "properly the Author of the Dunciad" (II.523). Moreover, there seem to have occurred some significant changes in the poem as it took shape. Writing to Swift at an early stage of the project, before Swift had become deeply involved in it—and shortly before that rash of letters in which the poet protested so about his honesty—Pope comments that Ambrose Philips' failure to achieve preferment will "spoil a very good conclusion to one of my Satyrs, where having endeavour'd to correct the Taste of the town in wit and Criticisme, I end thus.

> But what avails to lay down rules for Sense?
> In —— 's Reign these fruitless lines were writ,
> When Ambrose Philips was preferr'd for wit!" (II.332)

The passage sounds like an exasperated continuation of *An Essay on Criticism,* in the voice of that good man who once before had written with the positive aim of correcting the taste and judgment of the town. And when the line on Philips does appear, in almost the same form, in *The Dunciad,* it occurs as part of that concluding prophecy, by Settle, which I have said resembles Pope's established manner of speaking poetically for himself more than does any other portion of the poem. Begun by Pope, the poem on dulness was completed by an anti-Pope, prompted by the rankling Dean.

11. The Burden of the Present

Difficult as it is to write verse effectively at any time, it was especially difficult at the beginning of the eighteenth century for reasons lately set forth in several books. How dispiriting to be born "*immediately* after a great creative achievement,"[1] that of the Renaissance, culminating in the prodigious accomplishments of Milton. Ambitious to write epics, Dryden and Pope had to be content with translating them—a consideration which brings out the poignancy in Dryden's comparison of Homer, Virgil, and the author of *Paradise Lost:*

> The first in loftiness of thought surpass'd,
> The next in majesty, in both the last:
> The force of Nature could no farther go. . . .

Loftiness and majesty were scarce, for all but the hardiest kinds had been put to flight by that new empirical attitude toward the physical universe—as well as toward the mind, society, government, religion, ethics, learning, and literature—which variously characterized Newton and Locke, the Whigs, the Royal Society,

---

[1] W. Jackson Bate, *The Burden of the Past and the English Poet* (Cambridge, Mass., 1970), p. 12.

the new literate middle classes, and the emerging novelists. Instead of visions, optics. The amphibious Addison could imagine Publick Credit as the heroine of a rococo pageant, witness *Spectator* No. 3, but Defoe some ten years later, a decade after the publication of *Windsor-Forest*, would look hard at the Thames and find the nymphs departed.[2] The more-than-heroic grandeur of a Rubens ceiling which had exalted men's forebears now diminished those who walked so far down below it. No longer could a poet easily awe his readers with transcendent allegories, nor could he conveniently appropriate authority from allegiance with crown or cloth, though allusive affiliation with republican and Augustan Rome had some lasting force. Authority had to be earned, not through majesty but through refinement and also, if a poet's readership was to include more than the elite and parvenu, "honesty."[3]

Literary histories of the period could profit from increased imaginative identification with the poets, so much more alone

[2] *A Tour Thro the Whole Island of Great Britain*, ed. G. D. H. Cole (London, 1962), I, 173–76, cited by Isaac Kramnick, *Bolingbroke and His Circle* (Cambridge, Mass., 1968), pp. 196, 302.

[3] Rachel Trickett, in *The Honest Muse* (Oxford, 1967), stresses the "realistic," plain-speaking tendencies of Dryden, Pope, and other Restoration/eighteenth-century poets in an effort to counterbalance what she regards, rightfully I think, as overemphasis of the Renaissance world picture by recent commentators on their poems (pp. 14–15). Yet though writing very sensitively about stylistic, rhetorical effects, she may be thought to write too exclusively as a Modern: happily no historicist (as I use the term here), she may nevertheless seem insufficiently historical in her judgments. For example, she singles out Dryden's little poem on Oldham as his most powerful elegy, explaining that it imposes no apotheosis or consolation on readers (pp. 23–24). Comparably, she remarks that "the honest layman is the spokesman in *Religio Laici*. . . . Sincerity has to be taken for granted in a defense of the poet's religious faith like *The Hind and the Panther*" (p. 81). But sincerity (or, in the nonreligious sense, good faith) has to be taken for granted—that is, does not seem manifest in the latter poem itself as a whole—because the peculiar form of *The Hind and the Panther* is so questionably suited to the actualities of its time as they appear to later readers.

were they than most of their great predecessors—certainly so
much more conscious of their isolation, of the gaps between men,
and the walls. The dynamic Milton, though blind and compassed
round with dangers, could somehow write as if Descartes had not
existed, as if he himself were a part of some all but tangible corporation of minds, a member of a mystical body, drawn and quar-
tered though the palpable trunk had been in times of schism,
rebellion, regicide, and "restoration." Milton had the capacity,
and the privacy, to work up Pauline self-assurance; but for Dryden, the poet laureate committed to a public, political responsibility—as well as a self-supporting entrepreneur of poems and
plays—the problem of pleasing his audience was more insistent.
He grappled with it through most of his life. Still practically
Milton's contemporary, he could employ Scripture—to be sure,
the more outrightly historical books—as if it were literal history,
making the author of Samuel describe the Exclusion Crisis, the
account so persuasive because *Absalom and Achitophel* is formed as
if not by human hands: only incidentally by Dryden, the argument
of the poem proceeds from nature and Providence. In his epistles, especially *Religio Laici,* he had found a means of persuasion
beautifully suited to the needs and tastes of his contemporaries,
a *via media* for men neither irreligious nor fervent; "A man is to
be cheated into passion, but to be reason'd into truth," as he says
in the preface. But finally, under the unfortunate James II, in
The Hind and the Panther he made his ultimate commitment, more
Miltonic in purpose than in power. It is significant that he chose
the medieval form of beast fable to defend Roman Catholicism,
modified as the form was by his inclusion of extensive debate, for
a man is not ordinarily to be reasoned into acceptance of mystery
and dogmatic authority. Like Milton during the Restoration,
Dryden after the Revolution of 1688 became a private person
writing apolitical verse, indulging himself in Virgil and old fables,

warming himself at Chaucer's hearth, and closing his canon in the utterly outmoded genre of masque.

The Glorious Revolution proved momentous in many ways, perhaps most momentous in that, whatever difficulties remained in its wake for dissenters and others, it went far toward making political and religious pluralism a permanent condition of English life. The laws of 1689, giving Parliament decided supremacy over the King in all important matters, at the same time—ostensibly, at worst—made persuasion and compromise the major instruments of political action, superseding or outweighing authority and obedience. Henceforth common sense would presumably rule the people through some of the people's representatives. England had to an extent, in Dryden's iterated words, been "drawn to the dregs of a democracy," and therefore the first consideration of every critic studying Dryden's immediate successors, Prior, Swift, Gay, Thomson, and Pope, ought perhaps to be this: that to succeed on a scale of any size these poets had to please people very different from themselves, people keenly conscious of the differences, defensive, and suspicious. Matthew Prior seems a remarkable example, so thorough in his more earnest works is the division between what he wrote primarily to attract others, much to the taste of the late seventeenth century, and what he wrote to satisfy himself; between the florid public odes and the grandiose *Solomon*, on the one hand, and, on the other, such potent, undecorated poems as "Jinny the Just" or "An Epitaph," or such essays as his *Dialogues of the Dead*. Pope, it is worth noting, warmly praised the unpublished dialogues in a conversation with Spence,[4] and in 1727 asked the Earl of Oxford for permission to print "that Epitaph on Jenny of Mr Priors," as yet unpublished, in the *Miscellanies* being compiled with Swift, who would find

[4] Joseph Spence, *Observations, Anecdotes, and Characters of Books and Men Collected from Conversation*, ed. James M. Osborn (Oxford, 1966), I, 92.

the addition of Prior's poem "very agreable" (II.466). The Dean, after his early flirtation with Pindarics, had no patience with nymphs and muses.

One may profitably compare Dryden's firm commitment to Roman Catholicism with Pope's comparatively casual adherence, Dryden's sober arguments in *The Hind and the Panther* with Pope's statement (I.453–54) that at an early age he read a succession of Protestant and Catholic tracts from James's days, agreeing alternately with each position.[5] Pope's suppleness might well be described as a kind of pluralism of personality. In the political climate of 1689 and after, each man was potentially a source of wisdom and no man the exclusive source, society resting in principle upon the open-minded, modest contributions of many voices attempting to find truth and agreement. Above all forms, the essay in this climate flourished, in the spirit of Bacon and Locke and Montaigne, who wrote to practical, unfanatical, civic-minded men. Locke, as befitted the defender of the Revolution, had begun his monumental, emancipive *Essay Concerning Human Understanding* with the confession that he wrote not to "men of large thoughts and quick apprehensions; to such masters of knowledge I profess myself a scholar, and therefore warn them beforehand not to expect anything here, but what, being spun out of my own coarse thoughts, is fitted to men of my own size, to whom, perhaps, it will not be unacceptable that I have taken some pains to make plain and familiar to their thoughts some truths which established prejudice, or the abstractness of the ideas themselves, might render difficult." Comparably, Mr. Spectator hoped to bring "Philosophy out of Closets and Libraries, Schools and Colleges, to dwell in Clubs and Assemblies, at Tea-Tables and in Coffee-Houses." And in the early 1730s Voltaire, for the benefit

---

[5] Earl Miner documents Dryden's comparatively thorough familiarity with the same materials, in *John Dryden's Poetry* (Bloomington, 1967), p. 191.

of his trammeled countrymen, could describe the results of these and other efforts in education as if he had just returned from Periclean Athens: "The *English* generally think, and Learning is [held] in greater Honour among them than in our Country; an Advantage that results naturally from the Form of their Government. There are about eight hundred Persons in *England* who have a Right to speak in publick, and to support the Interest of the Kingdom; and near five or six Thousand may in their Turns, aspire to the same Honour. The whole Nation set themselves up as Judges over these, and every Man has the Liberty of publishing his Thoughts with regard to publick Affairs; which shews, that all the People in general are indispensably oblig'd to cultivate their Understandings. In *England* the Governments of *Greece* and *Rome* are the Subject of every Conversation, so that every Man is under a Necessity of perusing such Authors as treat of them, how disagreeable soever it may be to him; and this Study leads naturally to that of polite Literature"[6] — a nation of essayists.

What was a poet to do? Conventions were suspect, parties and sects divisive. There was no royal road. He could content himself with technical mastery, in pastorals wavering self-consciously between seriousness and satire, in an aria like *Messiah*, in a secular Revelation like *Windsor-Forest* or a tour de force like *The Rape of the Lock.* He could be a boy forever in such ingenuous if skillful poems, a virtuoso, a prodigy. He could translate, edit: become a curator. In bitterness he could find relief in brilliant, anonymous ventriloquism, as in *The Dunciad.* Having made his fortune he

[6] *Letters Concerning the English Nation. By Mr. De Voltaire* (London, 1733), pp. 193–94. This, the first edition of what later became known as the *Lettres philosophiques*, was translated by John Lockman. Voltaire's thinking was not so wishful as it sounds; for a positive, anti-Namierite view of the range and power of eighteenth-century opinion, limited as the franchise was, see J. H. Plumb, "Political Man," in *Man Versus Society in Eighteenth-Century Britain* (Cambridge, 1968), ed. James L. Clifford, pp. 1–21.

could retire. Or he could, as Pope did, find a way of speaking to
his times, not appropriating so much as generating the requisite,
personal authority, along lines not very different from those he
admired in the early work of Voltaire, "who . . . is not less a Poet
for being a Man of Sense." Having received from Bolingbroke a
copy of *La Ligue* (later retitled the *Henriade*), Pope replied with
appreciative criticism and more: "Do not smile when I add, that I
esteem him for that honest principled Spirit of true Religion
which shines thro' the whole; and from whence (unknown as I
am to Mr de Voltaire) I conclude him at once a Free thinker and a
Lover of Quiet; no Bigot, but yet no Heretick: one who honours
Authority and National Sanctions without prejudice to Truth or
Charity; One who has Study'd Controversy less than Reason, and
the Fathers less than Mankind; in a word, one worthy from his
rational temper of that share of Friendship & Intimacy with which
you honour him" (II.229). Not the best description of Voltaire;
but in a mold somewhat like this, Pope would within ten years
felicitously recast his own poetic person, though as someone
other than a narrator of epic verse.

12. Overtures to Love

"Remember," the exiled Atterbury warned Pope in a letter of 1729, "Virgil dy'd at 52, and Horace at 58; and, as bad as both their Constitutions were, Yours is yet more delicate and tender. Employ not your precious Moments, and great Talents, on little Men, and little things: but choose a Subject every way worthy of you; and handle it, as you can, in a manner which no body else can equal, or imitate" (III.77). About a year earlier, as if *The Dunciad* had never been written, Swift remarked to the poet that "with regard to particular men, you are inclin'd always rather to think the better, whereas with me it is always directly contrary. I hope however, this is not in you from a superior principle of virtue, but from your situation, which hath made all parties and interests indifferent to you, who can be under no concern about high and low-church, Whig and Tory, or who is first Minister" (II.497). In the 1730s, particularly the earlier of those years, as if to comply with Atterbury and to refute Swift, Pope turned to new matter and manner, in *An Essay on Man*, the *Moral Essays*, and the *Imitations of Horace* (the Virgilian hope gone), and began to season his more informal verse with political commentary—as if he had finally become a fully fledged British citizen. In 1714, at the

Queen's death, he had sided with certain Tories, but chiefly because they were his close friends (p. 79) and because the Whigs
were the more anti-Catholic party. Now, in the thirties, he would
become identified with the Opposition to Sir Robert Walpole, the
"first Minister."

Opposition to Pope on the part of the Dunces remained vehe-
ment. Writing to Broome, who had resentfully stopped corres-
ponding with his former employer, Elijah Fenton commented
in 1729: "The war is carried on against him furiously in pictures
and libels; and I heard of nobody but Savage and Cleland who
have yet drawn their pens in his defence. He told me that for the
future he intended to write nothing but epistles in Horace's manner, in which I question not but he will succeed very well"
(III.37): a sound prediction. In the various epistles of the early
and mid-thirties, however, Pope did not simply avoid further
skirmishes with the Dunces; he created for himself a public character formidable enough to withstand, ingratiating enough to dis-
arm, all but the most assiduous calumny. The project may be said
to have begun feebly in the notes to *The Dunciad* that fill the
Variorum edition of 1729, seemingly designed to humanize the
negative narrator.[1] And the project continues in Pope's efforts,
laborious as they were devious, to recall and publish his letters,
a task that (to judge by the amount of space which talk of it takes
up in the *Correspondence*) may in the end have been as time-con-
suming as translating the *Odyssey*. To reconstruct oneself publicly
is a considerable task, eased as it must have been for Pope by a
degree of economic security he had not always felt—seldom does
he mention money in his letters now—and a social position he
must have coveted in his youth. Now young poets, such as James

[1] As Aubrey L. Williams suggests in remarking that the notes tend "to establish
a *persona*, that of a 'good man,' for the poet" (*Pope's "Dunciad": A Study of Its Meaning* [London, 1955], p. 79).

Thomson and David Mallet, brought him their work. Come of age, the protégé had become a patron, though still himself patronized companionably by lords, Bathurst, Burlington, and others, Pope's peers.

Most significant of all: in prelapsarian times Pope had gone riding in Windsor Forest with Trumbull, a retired secretary of state, their conversations on the classics serving as the young poet's college; now, after Bolingbroke had returned from exile and settled, in 1725, at Dawley Farm, Pope could begin to regain intimacy with a statesman in retirement, but on terms better than before, since Bolingbroke was resoundingly a more remarkable man than the elderly knight. A dynamic patrician still covertly very active in politics (the "anti-Minister," Walpole called him in 1734), Bolingbroke was fascinatingly erudite, full-brained with intellectual projects, and, best of all, not Pope's patron so much as his friend. In the Viscount, Pope found not a parent but an elder brother; in the early thirties they constituted a freemasonry of two; and—almost—what Swift was to *The Dunciad,* Bolingbroke was to nearly all Pope's later poetry. If Trumbull was Pope's tutor, Bolingbroke was his senior colleague.

Bolingbroke could claim, as he did in a letter to Swift, that *An Essay on Man* was begun "att my instigation" (III.213), and Spence records Pope's account of beginning the first of the Horatian imitations after Bolingbroke had casually suggested a translation.[2] On the other side, Pope could boast to Swift early in 1732, "It is the greatest vanity of my life that I've contributed to turn my Lord Bolingbroke to subjects moral, useful, and more worthy of his pen" than political ephemera (III.276). What might not these two and Swift accomplish if reunited! On the same page Pope says, "I fancy if we three were together but for three years,

[2] Joseph Spence, *Observations, Anecdotes, and Characters of Books and Men Collected from Conversation,* ed. James M. Osborn (Oxford, 1966), I, 143.

some good might be done even upon this Age; or at least some
punishment made effectual, toward the Example of posterity."
Dawley Farm lying within a few miles of Pope's villa, the poet
could often see his guide, philosopher, and friend, and could thus
give Swift a running account of Bolingbroke's projects, exciting
at the time whatever their issue. In May, 1733, Bolingbroke is
studying metaphysics, about to turn to history (iii.372–73). In
September, 1734, Pope pleads lightheartedly, "Permit me to wear
the beard of a philosopher, till I pull it off, and make a jest of it
myself. 'Tis just what my Lord B. is doing with Metaphysicks.
I hope, you will live to see and stare at the learned figure he will
make, on the same shelf with Locke and Malbranche." To the
letter Bolingbroke adds a postscript: "It is true I have writ six
letters and a half to him on subjects of that kind, and I propose
a letter and a half more which would swell the whole up to a considerable volume" (iii.433). Swift replies that from this time forward he will write to both in the same letters, saving money and
time—"And he being your *Genius*," he tells Pope, "no matter to
which it is addressed" (iii.440). This period of happy intimacy
ended, though, in 1735, when Bolingbroke went to live in France,
having become an embarrassment to the Opposition once Walpole
had attacked him openly as its leader. But during this period
Pope had written and published *An Essay on Man*, the *Moral Essays*, and half the *Imitations*, and Bolingbroke had published his
Remarks on the History of England and his *Dissertation upon Parties*.
More was expected: in 1740 Pope wrote to Bolingbroke, "The
greatest vanity I have is to see finished that noble work, which
You address to me, & where my Verses, interspersed here &
there, will have the same honour done them to all Posterity as
those of Ennius in the Philosophic writings of Tully" (iv.261).
When George, Lord Lyttelton told Pope that "You, and He have
Engrost Philosophy, Poetry, Antiquity, and Modern History"
(iv.348), leaving Lyttelton only the Middle Ages to range in, did

it seem like flattery? To the last Pope marvels at the abilities of
"my Great (truly Great) Friend" (IV.400), who was to stand weep-
ing by the dying poet's chair.

Inevitably, Bolingbroke became prominent in his friend's poems, as we have already seen in the two quotations, from *An
Essay on Man* and *The First Epistle of the First Book of Horace Imitated*, which occupy me in the initial pages of this portrait: "Come
then, my Friend, my Genius, come along . . ." and "You laugh,
half Beau half Sloven if I stand. . . ." Together the passages epito-
mize that blend of respect and familiarity which characterized the
friendship and served as a point of departure for the poet's philosophy. The first passage, in the formal setting of the *Essay*, refers
back especially to the cardinal lines opening the second epistle,
the lines on "this isthmus of a middle state." There the emphasis
is pessimistic, stress falling on the hazards of man's position between God and the beasts, the doubts, errors, vulnerability af-
flicting him. The lines at the end of the poem, which I have
quoted above, complement the earlier passage by stressing positive possibilities, of dignity, temper, relative but substantial
autonomy. As for the quotation from the epistle to Bolingbroke,
it too points backward, to earlier lines in that poem, lines of self-
portraiture:

> But ask not, to what Doctors I apply?
> Sworn to no Master, of no Sect am I:
> As drives the storm, at any door I knock,
> And house with Montagne now, or now with Lock.
> Sometimes a Patriot, active in debate,
> Mix with the World, and battle for the State,
> Free as young Lyttelton, her cause pursue,
> Still true to Virtue, and as warm as true:
> Sometimes, with Aristippus, or St. Paul,
> Indulge my Candor, and grow all to all;
> Back to my native Moderation slide,
> And win my way by yielding to the tyde.   (ll. 23–34)

This again is an abundantly complex passage, seemingly an assertion of complete independence and even a whimsical exercise of freedom, yet hardly that: whether one houses with Montaigne or Locke, one is in a reputable house, and though to dwell with either is to be attentive particularly to the value of one's own experience and thinking as distinguished from received wisdom, yet the other figures mentioned—especially Lyttelton and St. Paul (Lyttelton would later write a treatise on Paul's conversion) —indicate that the poet has not chosen an empiricism or rationalism divorced from ideals, or ideals unrelated to actualities; the attitude befits "One who has study'd . . . the Fathers less than Mankind." The zealous apostle had himself preached moderation, urging that it be shown to "all men" (Philippians 4:5), and had, he said, been made "all things to all men" (1 Corinthians 9:22). Living like hospitable Pope in "his own hired house," he had "received all that came in unto him" (Acts 28:30). What is more, for Pope to combine St. Paul with Aristippus, the philosopher of immediate pleasure and, as the Twickenham editor observes, the favorite philosopher of Bolingbroke—called Aristippus by Swift at one place in the *Correspondence* (III.29)—is to establish a point of view more plural than monocular.

The poet who, in the early poems, usually allowed himself a few lines of autobiography near the end now fills his work with self-description, apparently opening himself to all men, often colloquially, and the self is rich in plain human qualities which have come to the fore while more abstract matters have receded. The later poems do not stress soothing notions like that of the *concordia discors.* Seen from a certain altitude the world may appear orderly, but the man of, preeminently, the Horatian imitations has stooped to truth and speaks in and out of the welter of experience, his feet on the ground. Although Nature enters discreetly at a holy, ancient moment of *An Essay on Man,* the likes of

Father Thames do not lift their heads in the poems of the thirties; yet the poet has not forsaken the ideals such personages evoke, only depressed them, moved them to the background, where they may be said to belong in a period when they have lost their power over a poet's audience, perhaps over his mature mind. St. Paul and Moderation are still important, though not so important as the question of connecting them with one's own experience in a world that no longer takes their significance for granted. Though a believer, the poet lives in a time of doubt when men look for reasons, evidence; not imprudently, if one considers the strife of preceding centuries. Etiology, teleology—what history says man has been, what religion says he must become—how may the strands be joined? The poet knows he cannot splice them in any permanent, perfectly persuasive way, so he looks at things both ways from the only really available vantage point, that of the transient present. It may be suggested that Pope, after the wreck of whatever ambition he may have had to emulate Virgil in pastoral, georgic, and epic, recognized that the bard of his time could be no more than an essayist, in morals, religion, philosophy, and politics, as well as in art.

What English poet before Pope says so much about himself and his actual, everyday circumstances? Not in the conspicuously rhetorical, aprioristic, elitist *Essay on Man* (Oh for a closer walk with Bolingbroke) but in the conversational *Moral Essays,* with their attempt to reconcile morality and empirical psychology, and especially in the *Imitations,* despite their Horatian origin primarily English, original poems. Exercises in self-representation, the latter pieces compare with Montaigne, descriptive as well as judgmental, as experiential as prescriptive, both humorous, directed against the speaker himself, and satirical. Not a saint, the speaker has to work himself up to his occasional heroism (hence the importance of transitions between personae, for intimacy might be described behavioristically as the condition in which a person lets another see him shifting roles), and he requires neither sainthood nor constant virtue of his readers. His hero Bolingbroke is subject to the vapors, is not ague-proof. Only in the *Epilogue to the Satires*, the one satire in which Pope represents himself as speaking to someone actively unsympathetic with his point of view, does the poet take a hard line throughout.

Useful as the concept of the persona or "mask" is to rhetorical analysis, it must not conceal from us a man who, with more dedication than any English poet before him, tried to speak out of his own quotidian life in an attempt to win the love of his readers by being, as much as possible, convincingly himself. The strategy, if that is not too calculating a word, is put simply in a letter to Swift dating from 1729: "I lately receiv'd . . . several of my own letters of about fifteen or twenty years old; and it was not unentertaining to my self to observe, how and by what degrees I ceas'd to be a witty writer; as either my experience grew on the one hand, or my affection to my correspondents on the other. Now as I love you better than most I have ever met with in the world, and esteem you too the more the longer I have compar'd you with the rest of the world; so inevitably I write to you more negligently, that is more openly, and what all but such as love another will call writing worse" (III.79). The thought is not a new one, or new to Pope; for example, he had said as much to Caryll in 1712, offering the same negligent openness as a proof of epistolary sincerity (I.155). But in the *Moral Essays* and the *Imitations* he offered himself thus to the public, generally in public letters to his friends; and his friends, who knew him as he actually was, found no remarkable flaws in his self-portrayal. Perhaps the social and political implications of Pope's manner may best be suggested by a sociologist's description of exalted persons, who "become so sacred that the only fitting appearance they can make is in the center of a retinue and ceremony; it may be thought improper for them to appear before others in any other context, as such informal appearances may be thought to discredit the magical attributes imputed to them."[3] Elaborate, formal staging of the self becomes a major complaint against Addison in the *Epistle to Dr. Arbuthnot;* allowing no rival near the throne, presiding over the Buttonian little senate of sycophants, Atticus differs completely from the unceremonious, palpably human poet who is trying to pull himself together in the familiar setting of his own home — a poet, moreover, who in this poem, an epistle not based on any of Horace's, is being himself still more thoroughly than in most of the satires.

A recent study of the *Imitations* demonstrates a fusion of Horace and Christianity which Pope accomplished with the aid of the pagan poet's Christian commentators;[4] but that stratum lies beneath the poems, in the background, a matter of allusion. In the foreground stands the self-conscious, to that extent isolated poet, concerned as he sanely is with the things about him: friends, passersby, houses and gardens, enemies, pests, acts of Parliament, current events, the food on his plate, the glass in his hand; doing commonplace things: complaining to Arbuthnot, consulting a

[3] Erving Goffman, *The Presentation of Self in Everyday Life* (Garden City, N.Y., 1959), p. 120.

[4] Thomas E. Maresca, *Pope's Horatian Poems* (Columbus, Ohio, 1966). Introducing an account of the religious basis of the third *Moral Essay*, Earl R. Wasserman observes, "Although the persistent Christian resonances in the poem identify his religious commitment, the main speaker concedes, as a rhetorician should, to adapt his discourse to the character of his immediate audience, the worldly, cynical nonbeliever — the persona here named 'Bathurst'" (*Pope's "Epistle to Bathurst": A Critical Reading with an Edition of the Manuscripts* [Baltimore, 1960], p. 12) — a comment applicable, with some qualification, to the author/audience relationship in much of Pope's verse of the thirties.

lawyer, eating with Swift, and so forth. Cognizant, certainly, of
the secular and sacred history of temporal things and events, he
is *as* aware, at least, of the gap between ordinary matters and the
forms of mind and conscience that attach to them. Able to give
himself exclusively to neither, as a poet he gives himself to both
in the hope of securing respect and affection, and with them a
basis for social, ultimately political harmony, depending on his
own judgment to avoid mental dismemberment. It was not an easy
position to sustain; what made it endurable for him was perhaps
a newly receptive sense of time, especially of time as a succession
of relatively discrete moments promoting and embracing change,
ebb, and flow, the tide of what I have called his pluralism. The
two imitations of Donne, begun before the translation of Homer
and revised before their publication in 1735, certainly imply a
change in Pope's sensibility. In contrast to the Horatian imitations, they remain declamatory in form, are addressed to no one
in particular, make no mention of Twickenham and its paraphernalia, and contain but a scattering of references to historical people and events. Both versions of Donne, moreover, emphatically
portray life as a prelude to eternity, Purgatory, Heaven and Hell,
revealing an eschatological sense of time not prominent in the
other imitations.

Are Pope's the genteel liberal views of a secure, successful man,
nurtured by the self-deception of an egotist? Yes, undoubtedly,
to some extent, though comparison with the personae of some of
his contemporaries will temper such judgments. Commentators,
notably Johnson, have been astringent on the subject of Pope's
candor, particularly with respect to his letters as he prepared
them for the public. In the *Life of Pope* Johnson remarks that only
children open their hearts to others, few men dare be candid with
themselves — though Johnson added, "The writer commonly be-

lieves himself,"[5] whatever value that concession may have. Pope's Pope in the later poems could not be, in every respect, the Pope that Pope himself was. The portrait does require qualification. But to the extent that such qualification obscures the poet's positive efforts toward accurate self-description, and the relative success of his achievement (even if one suspects that he sometimes made himself into a person whom he could candidly reveal), the commentator, whether he be historicist or formalist, betrays his subject. In the poems of the thirties, more than he or any English poet—perhaps more than any poet—had done before, Pope brought his poetical persona into close, relatively comprehensive alignment with the man we know from all biographical details. It was earlier in his career, and later, that the persona badly betrayed the man.

Close as Pope stood in these years to flamboyant Bolingbroke, he was not swallowed up but preserved independence, remained,

---

[5] *Lives of the English Poets,* ed. George Birkbeck Hill (Oxford, 1905), III, 207–8. In the course of a symposium on "The Concept of the Persona in Satire"—a watershed of the controversy—that appeared in *Satire News Letter,* Vol. III (1966), Howard D. Weinbrot helpfully comments on Johnson's views of Pope's self-presentation in the letters and the *Epistle to Dr. Arbuthnot.* The letters disappoint because "the pose is *too* far from the man," while the poem pleases because Pope's somewhat idealized self-portrait does not misrepresent the generally good man that Pope was; and hence, "the criterion of reasonable appropriateness in considering the mask which refers to the man behind it, may suggest one way of reconciling the demands of the persona and the biographical critics" (p. 144). I would add, however, that one must peer hard at Johnson's remarks on *Arbuthnot* to perceive a distinction between the speaker of the poem and the historical Pope. And, allowing that the mask was a recognized literary device in Pope's time, one might even argue the highly speculative point that the eighteenth century, more than other eras, permitted virtual unification of mask and self because authors were relatively free of the political and social restraints which earlier had inhibited candid self-description, while psychology had not yet revealed complexities too numerous for any realistic mask to comprehend.

perhaps finally became, his own person, as inconsistent and inadequate as he sometimes confessed himself to be. If comparison
of his new public character with another's is helpful, I may mention the unglamorous yet in some ways attractive character of, not
certainly Bolingbroke, but the "Trimmer" whom the Marquess
of Halifax—that statesman whose stability helped smooth the
course of the Revolution—described in a famous pamphlet published just before the flight of the unyielding James II. Like Pope,
Halifax admired Montaigne, deeply, and enunciated a political
philosophy of considerable flexibility—a politics of the possible—
that matches the social attitudes of Pope's Horatian spokesman,
a philosophy based like that of Pope's satires upon principles of
honesty, tolerance, and, above all, affection. What Halifax says
of the king fits Pope's satirist as well: "He who feareth the King,
only because he can punish, must wish there were no King; so that
without a principle of Love, there can be no true Allegiance, and
there must remain perpetual Seeds of Resistance against a power
that is built upon such an unnatural Foundation, as that of fear
and terrour."[6]

Perhaps a sentimental notion. But like the Pope who, as Johnson
says, could not drink tea without a stratagem, Halifax was a
tough-minded man, given to maxims such as these: "Friendship
cannot live with Ceremony, nor without Civility"; "A Man is to go
about his own Business as if he had not a Friend in the World to
help him in it"; "The most useful Part of Wisdom is for a Man to

---

[6] George Savile, first Marquess of Halifax, *Complete Works,* ed. Walter Raleigh
(Oxford, 1912), p. 57. For Halifax's devotion to Montaigne, see p. 185. Maynard
Mack has noted that Pope's relation to Montaigne deserves further study (*The
Garden and the City: Retirement and Politics in the Later Poetry of Pope, 1731-1743*
[Toronto, 1969], p. 234*n*); a short account of sources and analogues may be found
in E. Audra, *L'Influence française dans l'œuvre de Pope* (Paris, 1931), pp. 466–80.

give a good guess, what others think of him."[7] How much the first
maxim resembles Pope's poetic representation of his friendship
with Bolingbroke, and how much the latter maxims recall statements late in the *Correspondence*, for example Pope's remark to
Martha Blount "that of all the Princes in Europe I admire the
King of Prussia, because he never tells any body any thing he intends to do" (IV.212)—the letters are remarkable for their paucity
of information about his poems—or this declaration made to
Ralph Allen: "No true Judgment can be made, here, of any Man or
any Thing, with certainty; further, than that we *think* another
man means well, and that we *know* we ourselves mean well. It
is in this Situation that every honest man stands with respect to
another, and upon which all well-principled Friendships depend"
(IV.479). Pope's personality did not change utterly in the early
thirties, his letters remaining full of disingenuous ingenuousness:
he equivocates with Caryll so as to procure an unbiased opinion
of *An Essay on Man* (III.354), he tricks Curll with pseudonymous
communications of bogus autobiography (III.388), he goes to any
mendacious length to preserve secrecy, even with close friends,
in his scheme of publishing the letters. In fact, Pope's shrewdness
resembles Walpole's, though exercised in a smaller sphere; readers

[7] Halifax, pp. 243, 245, 255. One other passage might have been quoted as
especially significant to a man like Pope: "Temporal things will have their weight
in the World, and tho Zeal may prevail for a time, and get the better of a Skirmish,
yet the War endeth generally on the side of Flesh and Blood, and will do so till
Mankind is another thing than it is at present: And therefore a wise Papist in cold
Blood, considering these and many other Circumstances, which 'twill be worth
his pains to see if he can unmuffle himself from the Mask of Infallibility, will think
it reasonable to set his Imprison'd Senses at Liberty, and that he hath a right to see
with his own Eyes, hear with his own Ears, and judge by his own Reason" (p. 85).
Love, not authority, was the capstone of the poet's religion; as he had written to
Atterbury back in 1717, in one of his major religious *apologiae*, he thought himself
"not a Papist" but "a Catholick, in the strictest sense of the word" (I.454).

of Diderot may be reminded, by each in his element, of the hard, warm, wily père Hudson whose machinations enliven *Jacques le fataliste*—"le meilleur des amis et le plus dangereux des ennemis."[8]

It should be noted that at the turn of 1732–33 the poet was engaged in editing some papers of Halifax, the great-grandfather of his friend Lady Burlington, a task entailing work with the maxims I have quoted, and a process he regarded as "a Pleasure & Improvement to me" (III.341). Which is not to claim that Pope modeled himself on Halifax, but only to say that he was in touch with forceful English minds besides Bolingbroke's; the Pope of the thirties, unlike the Pope of the late twenties, cannot easily be defined by reference to Bolingbroke, Swift, or anyone else. It is also to suggest that his self-portrayal, like Halifax's portrait of the Trimmer, bore a positive, pragmatic relation to the exigencies of his untidy time. Only the mask of a real face would do. Although Pope put his best face forward, it was unquestionably, in detail, his own, despite concealment of some blemishes—the realistic if not in every respect real face of a poet who, in the *Imitations* particularly, tried to be himself more thoroughly and generously than he had in his earlier poems, the face of a vulnerable, conscientious man in a changing state, a man speaking from experience, not innocence.

The years 1733–37 were, generally speaking, Pope's halcyon period, though not uninterrupted by hardship and sorrow: recurrent illness, his mother's death in 1733, Arbuthnot's in 1735, the departure of Bolingbroke. No longer bound to his mother's side, he could spend summer months visiting his friends' great houses. The *Essay on Man*, published anonymously and acknowledged by its author only after its popularity became certain, was

[8] Maynard Mack compares Pope and Walpole as "mighty opposites" in chapter 6 of *The Garden and the City*.

as yet unattacked by the scholar Crousaz; while after the defeat in 1733 of Walpole's excise proposal, Cobham, Marchmont, Burlington, and Chesterfield joined the opposition party, at once strengthening it, liberalizing it, and increasing their friend Pope's involvement with it. True, Bolingbroke's power ended a year later when his attack on the Septennial Act failed, but after his return to France Pope fell in with the congenial Lyttelton and other Patriots, whose cause seemed promising. In 1735 the poet could gloat over a private triumph when the deceived Curll brought out the letters, thus justifying Pope's own edition of two years later, and in 1735 was published also a second volume of the *Works*, containing poems written since 1717. Finally, in 1737, Pope succeeded in recalling his letters to Swift; their great friendship would be thoroughly documented for posterity. Death and disagreement having broken some of the poet's ties, he now formed new ones, with Ralph Allen for example, and always he could depend upon Martha Blount's companionship.

His reputation secure despite his enemies, his hopes for his country sometimes brightening, his own private life relatively comfortable, in the five years between 1733 and 1737 he wrote or completed nearly all the *Imitations* except the *Epilogue to the Satires*, some ten witty, expansive, personal essays ranging in tone from the hale fellowship of Bethel's Sermon (*Sat.* ii.ii) to the contemptuous familiarity of the epistle *To Augustus*, pouring himself out as plain, almost, as Montaigne, and perhaps sometimes with as little effort: the first *Imitation* was, he said, "the work of two mornings" (iii.350), and others, if one may take his word for it, were composed almost as rapidly (iii.358, iv.33). More than before or after, the work and the man—the inner and outer man—were one.

13. Apocalypse Not Revelation

His "agreeable and instructive neighbour . . . gone" (IV.6), Pope concentrated on gardening and grottofying, yet found time to become still more active politically than before. In a letter of 1736 he told Swift he had grown friendly with some "young men," the Boy Patriots, "who look rather to the past age than to the present, and therefore the future may have some hopes of them" —an ominous, telling description. The cousins Lyttelton and Gilbert West, nephews of Lord Cobham, who—together with Lords Cornbury and Marchmont, and Sir William Wyndham and William Pitt—cultivated Frederick, the Prince of Wales, in opposition to George II and Walpole, were more remarkable for their idealism than for their political sagacity. The art of government was not to be acquired simply by their, in Pope's words, "contempt of Corruption" (IV.51); but high, dramatic sentiments seemed invigorating. Lyttelton wrote to Pope in October, 1738, urging him to pursue the Prince: "Be therefore as much with him as you can, Animate him to Virtue, to the Virtue least known to Princes, though most necessary for them, Love of the Publick; and think that the Morals, the Liberty, the whole Happiness of this Country depends on your Success." What a terrible responsibility to lay on one curved back! "If that Sacred Fire, which by You and other Honest Men has been kindled in his Mind, can be Preserv'd, we may yet be safe; But if it go out, it is a presage of Ruin, and we must be Lost. For the Age is too far corrupted to Reform itself; it must be done by Those upon, or near the Throne, or not at all" (IV.138–39). The public, unable to reform itself, must nevertheless be loved, and virtue is the hinge of government; otherwise, apocalypse. Of course, time would prove the conversation of such men as Lyttelton to be more histrionic than perspicacious. To Pope's credit, his reply to Lyttelton—the most detailed of his surviving letters on political affairs, unsigned— brings matters somewhat down to earth (IV.142–44) and reveals his disillusionment with some of the Patriots.

But even in dismay he could attempt to rally others with Lytteltonian strains, as for example in a letter to Marchmont of 1740: "You . . . cannot be impotent or useless if God shall please to save us. Unless it be his will to give us to destruction," Marchmont must be savior. "This is the least you may do; to keep Virtue & Honour alive, in the breasts of many Young Men who are to give them on to Posterity; and to dash the Forehead and shake the soul of Guilty Wretches, who else would intail their Profligacy on all future generations" (IV.273). Now or never, all or nothing: the final version of *The Dunciad* was written in this tone and state of mind. While preparing Book IV for publication, Pope told Hugh Bethel, he burned to draw "the whole polite world upon me, (as I formerly did the Dunces of a lower Species) as I certainly shall whenever I publish this poem. An Army of Virtuosi, Medalists, Ciceronis, Royal Society-men, Schools, Universities, even Florists, Free thinkers, & Free masons, will incompass me with fury: It will be once more, *Concurrere Bellum atque Virum.* But a Good Conscience a bold Spirit, & Zeal for Truth at whatsoever Expence . . .; these animated me, & these will Support me" (IV.377). Thus, allying himself with the March-monts and Lytteltons, Pope would seem to have returned, as a neophyte in a different walk of life, walking without the company of his philosopher and friend, to the absolutist's preferences that characterize his early poems. And his association from 1739 with William Warburton, the dexterous, opportunistic defender of the poet's faith in *An Essay on Man*, appointed chaplain to Prince Frederick in 1740,[1] cannot have retarded this movement. Much as Pope idolized Bolingbroke, he was never so submissive to the free-thinking lord as he showed himself, immediately, to his orthodox commentator in the astonishing words, "I know I meant just what you explain, but I did not explain my own meaning so well as you: You understand me as well as I do myself, but you express me better than I could express myself" (IV.171–172). Perhaps the most spontaneous and delightful moment in the *Correspondence* comes when the poet, angered by an affront to Martha, tells her "W. is a sneaking Parson, & I told him he flatterd" (IV.464).

Yet as it happened, Bolingbroke was not so far away in person or in spirit. Pope corresponded with him, and in July, 1738, the month that the second dialogue of the *Epilogue to the Satires* was published, Bolingbroke came back to spend, it turned out, almost a year near Pope while trying to sell Dawley Farm. With the vexations of exclusion from government, not to mention having to witness the ineptness of the Patriots, were coupled those of pandering to a vulgar moneyed merchant who seemed the most likely buyer. By 1738–39 Bolingbroke himself had understandably hardened his opinions in the manner of Pope and the more ideal-istic Patriots; it was at this time that he composed *The Idea of a Patriot King*, which now or later, in manuscript, he entrusted to Pope's keeping. No longer, as *The Idea* shows, does Bolingbroke have hopes that England's old aristocrats may save her. All is lost

[1] Robert W. Rogers, *The Major Satires of Alexander Pope* (Illinois Studies in Language and Literature, Vol. 40; Urbana, 1955), p. 98 (correcting *DNB*).

unless there appear a monarch wise but especially virtuous, that *deus ex machina* whom he, Pope, and the Patriots improbably located in Prince Frederick. At the Patriot King's accession, or manifestation, according to Bolingbroke's concluding prophecy, "Peace and Prosperity will appear thro' his Country; Joy in every Face, Content in every Heart; a People un-oppressed, undisturbed, unalarmed; busy to improve their Private Properties, and the Publick Stock; while their Fleets shall cover the Ocean, bringing home Wealth by the Returns of Industry, carrying Assistance or Terror abroad by the Direction of Wisdom, and asserting triumphantly thro' the World the Right and Honour of *Great Britain.*"[2] *Windsor-Forest* once more. That Pope was still latently receptive to such idealism, the *Epilogue* suggests and the unfinished, unpublished satire *One Thousand Seven Hundred and Forty* makes plain. It begins with criticism of the Opposition leaders and ends (perhaps uncertainly, "Alas, on one alone our all relies") with a celebration of Frederick: "Europe's just balance and our own may stand,/ And one man's honesty redeem the land."

[2] From the rare edition Pope printed without Bolingbroke's knowledge, the existence of which so enraged the nobleman when he discovered it after the poet's death; as quoted by Fannie E. Ratchford in "Pope and the *Patriot King*," *Texas Studies in English*, No. 6 (1926), p. 177. Curiously, Bolingbroke's authorized version sounds still more like *Windsor-Forest:* compare "In Brazen Bonds shall barb'rous *Discord* dwell" (l. 414) with Bolingbroke's sentences just preceding the equivalent of those in my text, "Civil fury will have no place . . .: or, if the monster is seen, he must be seen as *Virgil* describes him, *Centum vinctus catenis/ Post tergum nodis, fremit horridus ore cruento.* He must be seen subdued, bound, chained, and deprived entirely of power to do hurt. In his place, concord will appear" (*Letters, on the Spirit of Patriotism: on the Idea of a Patriot King: and On the State of Parties, At the Accession of King George the First* [London, 1749], p. 225). Later editions correct *catenis* to *ahenis,* "brazen"; Dryden's translation of the pertinent phrase, from *Aeneid* I.295–96, is "bound in brazen chains." Bolingbroke, formerly "a good disciple of Lord Halifax," in the *Patriot King* departs from his master's principle that a king should be the servant of the people, according to Isaac Kramnick, *Bolingbroke and His Circle* (Cambridge, Mass. 1968), p. 34.

The last of the *Imitations* Pope published, the *Epilogue to the Satires* of 1738, is his farewell to Horace and to the genial, charitable relativism that warms and illuminates the series. "But *Horace*, Sir," Pope's Friend objects,

> was delicate, was nice;
> *Bubo* observes, he lash'd no sort of Vice:
> *Horace* would say, *Sir* Billy *serv'd the Crown*,
> Blunt *could do Bus'ness*, H—ggins *knew the Town*,
> In *Sappho* touch the *Failing of the Sex*,
> In rev'rend Bishops note some *small Neglects*,
> And own, the *Spaniard* did a *waggish thing*,
> Who cropt our Ears, and sent them to the King.   (Dial. 1.11–18)

The last reference, to the Spaniard who had clipped Captain William Jenkins' ear in 1731 and, as Pope has it in 1738, thereby had humiliated all England, will serve to introduce a final point on the subject of the poet's late moralism. For a long time Walpole had in his ignoble way kept England out of war and his opposition out of power, but by the year of Pope's *Epilogue*, as the first minister maneuvered toward a convention with Spain that might produce more years of peace, opponents were effectively challenging his alleged carelessness of the nation's honor. A major cause of friction was the Asiento signed at Utrecht which gave England control of the slave trade with the Spanish colonies, the abuse of which treaty had troubled Spain enough to make her rumble and harass British merchants. Walpole seemed committed to what those who underestimate the cost of war sometimes call a policy of peace at any price; in the long run, the Patriots' agitation would contribute to the sad, futile War of Jenkins' Ear (1739–41), to English involvement in the ensuing "world" War of the Austrian Succession, and to the fall of Walpole in 1742. One may note that in the imitation of Donne's fourth satire, published in 1735, Pope had put some cant about Spain's rapacity into the mouth of an obtuse courtier (l. 165). But three years later, as if rehearsing the concluding tableau of *The Dunciad*, he ends the first part of the *Epilogue* with a vision of Vice triumphant over court, mob, religion, and law; she

> Mounts the Tribunal, lifts her scarlet head,
> And sees pale Virtue carted in her stead!
> Lo! at the Wheels of her Triumphal Car,
> Old *England's* Genius, rough with many a Scar,
> Dragg'd in the Dust! his Arms hang idly round,
> His Flag inverted trails along the ground!

The point need not be labored; Pope was bidding beyond his means, and we have bought whatever sensitivity we have on the subject at too dear a price ourselves.[3]

Readers should not ignore that flicker of hopefulness I have sought to reveal in the latter, final *Dunciad* with its involved narrator and its comical notes to a dour text, Satire and History slightly trimming the sails of Pope's pessimism. Dim hopefulness of this sort was predicted by Lyttelton in an otherwise typical

[3] Kramnick comments, "The events of these years were forever a frightening example to Burke of the hazards created by outside pressure on the independent decisions of reasonable and wise legislators," and he quotes, and agrees with, a passage from Burke's *Letters on a Regicide Peace* which begins, "Sir Robert was forced into the war by the people who were enflamed to this measure by the most leading politicians, by their own orators and the greatest poets of the time. For the war Pope sang his dying notes" (p. 233). That Burke's comment was made in the atmosphere of the French Revolution need not detract from its accuracy; in quieter times the author of the first large-scale biography of Pope, Owen Ruffhead, had written of "the unhappy and unsuccessful war which a faction forced the nation into, in opposition to, and in order to destroy, Sir Robert Walpole" (*The Life of Alexander Pope* [London, 1769], p. 513). And although the War of the Austrian Succession was the major military result of the Patriots' agitation, it ought not to distract us entirely from the War of Jenkins' Ear; that conflict, despite its ludicrous name, was no laughing matter—as anyone acquainted with the horrors of the siege of Cartagena, made readily available by Tobias Smollett in *Roderick Random*, will certainly agree.

letter to Pope of November, 1741, a few months before the publication of the fourth book: how Lyttelton wishes Bolingbroke
were with them "to Exhort and Animate You not to bury your
excellent Talents in a Philosophical Indolence, but to Employ
them, as you have so often done, in the Service of Virtue. The
Corruption, and Hardness of the present Age is no Excuse; for
your Writings will Last to Ages to come, and may do Good a
thousand years hence, if they can't now; but I beleive they
wou'd be of great Present Benefit" (IV.369). Yet one cannot forget
that the lines from the *Epilogue to the Satires* were written by the
same man who, while celebrating the end of a war, several months
before the signing of the Asiento, had defined the gradations of
peace in *Windsor-Forest;* a man who had, over the years, brought
the visionary description of a peaceful life, as lived in the early
poem by a forest recluse, to realistic actualization in satires de-
picting the circumstances of a citizen living at Twickenham.
Though the triumph of Vice is alarming, I for one am a little
pleased to see Virtue carted off.

Part 3. Pope's "Proper Character"

—————◆—————

It is easy, after our experience of seemingly endless war, to write harshly about Pope's late poems promoting the wars that brought down Walpole and, more cruelly, many smaller men. Considering the formal merits of those poems, some readers may think it a mistake to emphasize Pope's warmongering— think it a rather Johnsonian confusion of aesthetics with thought in categories best kept separate from aesthetics: like Johnson's strictures on Pope's *Pastorals*. In the first part of the tripartite *Life of Pope*, basically a chronological account of the poet's public career, Johnson commends the *Pastorals* as remarkable offshoots of a youthful brain; but later, in the third, critical part of the *Life*, he expresses himself more firmly and typically: "It seems natural for a young poet to initiate himself by Pastorals, which, not professing to imitate real life, require no experience, and, exhibiting only the simple operation of unmingled passions, admit no subtle reasoning or deep enquiry."[1]

Examined chiefly with respect to their nice interrelations, or with respect to the tradition of pastoral, the poems are graceful

[1] *Lives of the English Poets*, ed. George Birkbeck Hill (Oxford, 1905), III, 101, 226. Subsequent parenthetical references are to this edition.

and mildly attractive. Even Johnson could remark that they are thoughtfully put together, with a correspondence of the times of day, the seasons, and the ages of man. A modern critic, enjoying *carte blanche* privileges with the riches of Renaissance Christian humanism, can extend the series to include the Golden through Iron Ages and much more, trying to see in the poems a world which, as the Twickenham editors say, answers to man's needs. But the world of the *Pastorals* does not—unless we think of them as contemporary with Spenser or Milton, as written in a still sacramental England. On the surface, the *Pastorals* are what T. S. Eliot, in *Four Quartets*, would call "a periphrastic study in a worn-out poetical fashion," and no one would read them today if their author did not go on to write much better. Yet beneath the surface, as I have argued in the first part of this essay, if the *Pastorals* are set not just against the tradition of such poems (which does, however, hint at contrasts) but also against the actualities of post-revolutionary England, with its secular, pluralistic, and realistic currents of thought, then Pope's series will be seen to dramatize the anguish of transition from a world of divine immanence, where a muse would visit her poet nightly, to a bleaker world where men would lie awake trying to imagine how they might reconcile themselves to their lonely condition. Pope wrote the *Pastorals* as if he could will himself back into an earlier period of literary history.

The surface of the poems sparkles with minute traditional perfections, but if a reader looks deeper he will be struck by the anomalies I have emphasized: the, when you realize it, overwhelming, ominous incongruity that exists between Pope's innocents, their unsympathetic and even hostile world—from which they persist in expecting comfort—and their helpless, evanescent narrator. Formal, mythopoetic analysis can emphasize the superficial beauties of the poems, their cleverness, drawing readers into a narrow world made somewhat more spacious by allusion but nevertheless static, timeless, and ahistorical. Biographical and historical considerations, however, enable a reader to sense the emotional action and force of the poems, which the poems are finally too flimsy to contain. Speculation on such historical grounds does not violate the form of the poems; it saves the poems from the constraints of their form. Or, to put the matter in a more sophisticated way, historical insight lets us realize how thoroughly the actual form of the poems differs from their apparent form, from what a connoisseur of pastorals must conventionally expect to find in examples of the genre, whatever their date, and probably will find in Pope's if he abandons himself to them as products of the Renaissance pastoral tradition. Johnson's refusal to settle for lesser worlds, the associative demands of his sensibility, make his old, sometimes slapdash criticism seem still forceful and fresh, to the point as we may finally feel the point of studying literature, its capacity to put us in touch with persons in history like ourselves, human voices still resonant through literature—persons by whom, out of their works and out of what else we can learn about them, we fashion, whether we will it or not, part of our sense of the limitations and possibilities of human existence.

Johnson went about the task un-self-consciously, directly, as if there could be no question about not only its worth and practicability but also its inevitability. The first and third parts of the *Life of Pope* Johnson joins with a second, middle part, a "character" of the poet that synthesizes his traits and constitutes the major intellectual feat of the whole biography, a veritable *tout comprendre.* Here, it seems, Johnson conjoins the disciplines of his multiple approaches to the poet, drawing the artist and the man into one person, into a critical focus enclosing both art and life. Johnson peels Pope's nature layer by layer, beginning with the outermost: "The person of Pope is well known not to have been formed by the nicest model" (III.196). Pope's chronic illness led to imperiousness and self-indulgence, and toward a delight in such artifices as would screen his weaknesses and demands. To compensate for his dependency, Pope craved thorough independence. "Having determined not to be dependent he determined not to be in want" (III.202)—Johnson will admit causality, and in fact, as the reader may suppose, how easily a "been" and a "had been" would slip in before those "determined's."

So Pope became extremely frugal, of money and of poetical ideas. He relished declarations of independence: he minimized the importance of his writing, to him; he pretended indifference to adverse criticism; he reveled in not just contempt of kings but wholesale *contemptus mundi*—and he shouldered the burdens of his dependent parents and his, in England, archaic religion, and he advertised his equality with the great, peers and authors. He became, for posterity, an artist of rare perfection; in art, "expecting no indulgence from others, he shewed none to himself" (III.221). He divided himself, or was divided: he snored in company, but in bed he lay awake rethinking his poems, hoarded his rhymes, and—with Swift—came close to what would now be diagnosed as paranoia: "He is afraid of writing lest the clerks of the Post-office should know his secrets; he has many enemies; he considers himself as surrounded by universal jealousy; 'after many deaths, and many dispersions, two or three of us,' says he, 'may still be brought together, not to plot, but to divert ourselves, and the world too, if it pleases'; and they can live together, and 'shew what friends wits may be, in spite of all the fools in the world.'" Says Johnson: "All this while it was likely that the clerks did not know his hand: he certainly had no more enemies than a publick character like his inevitably excites, and with what degree of friendship the wits might live very few were so much fools as ever to enquire" (III.211). In short, the "long disease" was not finally physical. Paranoia required megalomania; compensation for disabilities resulted in hypertrophy of Pope's poetical faculty and a certain general malignancy in his behavior.

In this character Johnson joins the biographical and critical first and third parts of the *Life*, it would seem. From a distance the character looks like an interdisciplinary triumph, but it is not; it is unidisciplinary. Not a word is said in the whole character about any of Pope's poems as in any sense informative about him. Instead we are given a remarkable, closed case history, both moral and psychological, which separates the man from the artist, drawing the artist's traits from the man's. Johnson judges the man—as distinguished from the artist—without respect to his works, like Calvin's God, and by Johnson's stern variety of eighteenth-century Christian moral standards the man seems in the main a selfish, calculating egotist—or would if Johnson did not seem to think of Pope as a person blindly overwhelmed by unconscious compulsions. In the character an environmentalist determinism struggles against traditional free-will ethics, and wins; and such an impression is reinforced by the retrospective cast of the character: the Pope Johnson describes is pointedly dead, everything in his life an accomplished fact—as, until his last moments, everything could not have appeared to Pope, and as the speaker of the poems cannot fully seem to a reader working his way through them.

By comparison, an interdisciplinary portrait of the poet, like the portrait attempted in the present essay, will not so exclusively distinguish the poet from the man, nor will it assume that one has a definite priority over the other. Such a portrait will find some degree of personal expression in the poems, even granting the premium an eighteenth-century poet placed on the public,

formal, traditional, and contrived aspects of poetry. Keeping
those qualities of eighteenth-century poetry in mind, the theorist
will seek a comparatively general formula. And seeking interdisciplinary insight he will lean lightly on his disciplines, allowing
none to attain an absolute status, lest he fall into a sort of ideological Calvinism like Johnson's, or like Christopher Caudwell's
Marxism. Moreover, looking for the living Alexander Pope, the
theorist will try to see his subject contemporaneously, not just
retrospectively, so as to preserve the elements of choosing and
groping that had to characterize the poet when he was alive. By
laboratory standards, the result will be a reconstruction of Pope
shot through from the start with various fallacies—that a reader
can sense a poet's intentions in his works, even intentions of which
the poet was probably not fully conscious; that a reader's own
responses tell him something real about what he is reading; that
biography has a direct, inevitable relation with literature. These
do present obstacles. For a long time the study of the humanities
proceeded as if these obstacles did not exist; for a while now,
the obstacles have seemed insuperable. The humanities, though,
can flourish at no extreme.

Looking for coherence in the career of Alexander Pope, a reader
may perceive two main curves of intellectual and emotional development, and the high points of that development signal Pope's
historic poetic and human achievements. The earlier poems,
those published between 1709 and 1717, proceed from an attempt
at naive conventionality in the *Pastorals,* rise to the shrewder idealism of *Windsor-Forest* and the bemused irony of *The Rape of the
Lock,* and then lapse into the sad if heroic alienation projected
upon *Eloisa to Abelard.* The curve of the later, post-Homeric poems, chronologically more condensed, takes Pope from the negative and positive authoritarianism of, respectively, the initial
Dunciad and *An Essay on Man,* to the plainer, more intimate style

and baroque-breaking substance of the *Moral Essays* and the *Imitations*, to the—again sad, again heroic—periods of the *Epilogue to the Satires* and the final, fourth book of *The Dunciad:* in a sense, a relapse, but certainly more than that too, as I shall argue before concluding.

With the early set of poems the Candidate for Fame finds a socially sanctioned voice, in general between *An Essay on Criticism* and *The Rape of the Lock*, a polite, public voice deriving its power from the secular, cosmopolitan manners of London in the years after the Revolution settlement: a brave world of possibilities for political cooperation. I do not write about *An Essay on Criticism* in Part 1 because it differs so from the other major poems of Pope's early years: it is not predominantly fictional and its speaker, unlike the observers of the other poems surrounding it in time, is a man in society—although, as befits an arbitrator, still a man somewhat aloof and on the whole carefully prudent, and very modest about himself at the end. Since the topic of this part of my essay includes not just Pope but his commentators as well, I will observe that the two major modern essays on the *Essay* almost fully illustrate the arc of Pope criticism in the past several decades, its partial vision and partial blindness. First came William Empson, a New Critic traveling light, with little besides a dictionary in his attaché case, to point out how many meanings the word *wit* has in the poem. Then came Edward Niles Hooker, a historicist with a wagonload of Pope's predecessors' writings—after Pope, only Empson's work—to explain how the *Essay* was related to the controversy in Pope's early years over whether wit could be made compatible with truth. Empson's vantage point is in the present, Hooker's is in the past. Both approaches are effective and one-sided.

Empson tries "to build a theory about the way complex meanings are fitted together in a single word, especially the 'key word' of a long poem." In *wit*, the key word of *An Essay on Criticism*,

Empson discerns a multiplicity of meanings ranging from social joking to judicious discourse, including those things themselves, the faculties producing them, and the persons with such faculties. The ambiguity of the word permits Pope to use it with great variety of denotation and connotation; Pope even satirizes his key word, "but without any hint that some other would be better; indeed no other would suggest so clearly that there is a hierarchy of literature which it would be ridiculous to peg down by terms." A hierarchy, that is, of discrimination, an order of classifying literature, extending from the broadest categories to the most subtle. "The cleverness of the thing is that the epigrams are ir-refutable if you stretch the meanings of the words far enough and give what the age demanded if you let them slip back."[2]

Empson's analysis is fine—as he says, it "improves the poem a great deal"—but it does not go far enough. Or, by implication, it goes too far, negatively. Empson concentrates entirely on the expressive and referential aspects of language, neglecting the aspect of communication. Words refer to things, the word *wit* to many things and combinations of things in the *Essay*, and words express the speaker's opinions and feelings in combination with his reference to things. But words are also addressed to an audi-ence and communicate expression and reference to that audience. This Empson does not take into account, or does so indirectly and ambivalently. Positively, he speaks of Pope's "deference to the democracy of the polite drawing room," adding that "such a view could only be made plausible if the drawing room were assumed to have a high standard; the strategy of Pope therefore made large demands on the 'common sense' which was to be made adequate to the task of criticism." Negatively, however, and more pervasively, Empson regards Pope's attempt to speak

2 William Empson, "Wit in the *Essay on Criticism*," *Hudson Review*, II (1950), 559, 570, 560.

to his age as a disabling limitation: the epigrams provide merely "what the age demanded if you let them slip back" to obvious meanings. The democracy of the poem is "a queer sort of democracy," a "drag toward the drawing room"[3] — in other words, elitist if not somehow unmasculine. But after all, any democracy discoverable in *An Essay on Criticism* would be likely to be odd, since democracy in the modern republican sense of the term had not yet been attempted or even invented. The government known to Pope was an oligarchy of birth and wealth, newly somewhat liberalized. The drawing room was a center of power. Beclouded by anachronistic expectations, Empson cannot perceive the political strength of the poem.

The important addition to be made to Empson's analysis concerns the political function of Pope's controlled ambiguity, Pope's achievement in giving the essential words breadth enough for more than one person to come in under them, space to accommodate both your sense of *wit* and mine — and Pope's deftness in giving that space a shape, guiding us toward forming *our* sense

[3] Ibid., pp. 560–61, 572. This prejudice hobbles Empson's reading of the best-known lines in the poem, "*True Wit* is *Nature* to Advantage drest,/ What oft was *Thought*, but ne'er so well *Exprest*." Empson comments, "Dr. Johnson, from whom sympathy might have been expected, thought the definition both false and foolish; novelty was not as unwelcome as all that; such an account of wit 'depresses it below its natural dignity, and reduces it from strength of thought to happiness of language.' This interpretation I think simply followed from having less respect for polite drawing rooms." Both interpretations, Empson's and Johnson's, seem to depend on too narrow a reading of the first line, which begins "*True Wit* is *Nature*" and thus implies that true wit is an aspect of nature, nature in a certain condition signified by proper dress, not the clothing alone. "This interpretation would not have occurred to me," says Empson, referring to a comparable gloss by Warburton (p. 573). But it should have: the next verse paragraph of the *Essay* reproves those who limit their attention to language "And value *Books*, as Women Men, for *Dress*"; and Empson's whole approach is based on the assumption that "the process of alternately identifying and separating a key pair of opposites is a fundamental one for the style" (p. 571).

of the word. The poem is a model of constructive political discourse. It is a literary constitution or social contract and a classic of communal speech, speech general enough to invite the untutored and, as Empson has shown, speech thoughtful enough to hold the expert. The *Essay* is oligarchic in tendency, as any realistic political statement had to be in 1711, but it is receptive as well as assertive. The poet's voice is the voice of a member of a pluralistic community, trying to draw the many into enhanced consciousness of what they may hold in common.[4] Variously ranging from the general to the specific, the poet catches in the word *wit* and other words not just a multiplicity of meanings but also a heterogeneous audience, of varying interests and capacities. Anyone taking the trouble to make historical comparisons, testing Empson's disparagement, will find that the *Essay* displays a decorum no more elitist than, say, Defoe's public although hardly proletarian voice in that very popular, pointedly political poem of 1701, *The True-Born Englishman.*

Hooker, on the other hand, does understand the political function of the *Essay's* language, describing the way Pope tried to bring together the partisans of wit and the partisans of learning and judgment, but, historicist that he is, he has in mind only the state of affairs in 1711. At the end of his article he explains Dryden's "definitions" of *wit* ("thoughts and words elegantly adapted to the subject," "a propriety of thoughts and words"). "Dryden was

[4] Maynard Mack has suggestively observed that the *Essay* shows a "warm concern for corporateness: for the relation of the individual, whether a man, an idea, a work of art, or a critical term, to a community, a One," but Mack's extremely elliptical remarks appeared, obscurely, in the introduction to an anthology for sophomores, *The Augustans* (2d ed.; Englewood Cliffs, N.J., 1961), p. 20. Although the introduction first appeared in 1950, there is no reference to it, and no stress on the point it makes, in the relevant volume of the Twickenham Edition, published eleven years later. The editors concentrate on historicist and mythopoeticist background.

urging a threefold relationship, between thoughts, words, *and* subject, effected in such a way that the three elements appear to belong to one another . . . ; and the words 'elegantly adapted' point to the need of an active literary intelligence to produce the work of *wit*."[5] What is left out, by Hooker if not by Dryden? Only the reader, yet few English poets have been, have had to be, as attentive to their reader as Dryden was. Or I should say their readers, since we too should be included, especially when the subject is Pope, who almost always had an eye on posterity— excessively, one may think regarding his Jeremian last poems. Hooker writes as if the object of literary scholarship were to find out what was happening two hundred years ago and let the matter rest at that. Like Empson, he does not think to explore the possibly enduring interest of the *Essay* as a classic of poetry meant to conjoin the perspectives of both an individual and a polis, as virtually the last such poem to have been written in English: the last fine poem we have that was written in an unalienated voice and the nearest model we have for public poetry if the writing of it ever again becomes possible.

To return to Pope's career: The cosmopolitan possibility fades for him with the accession of the first Hanoverian king; power comes to rest securely for many years with one comparatively Philistine party. The poet is cast upon himself: he must discover a generative way of speaking from political solitude, from more elementary human materials than those afforded by the earlier, in his view the more cohesive culture that nurtured his early work. The high point of the later series of poems occurs between the *Moral Essays* and the *Imitations of Horace*, with Pope's discovery

---

[5] "Pope on Wit: The *Essay on Criticism*," in *The Seventeenth Century: Studies in the History of English Thought and Literature from Bacon to Pope,* by R. F. Jones and Others Writing in His Honor* (Stanford, 1951; reissued 1965), p. 245.

of a less political than personal and social voice that, more deeply and more comprehensively than the voices of his English poetic predecessors, emanates from the poet's own daily, autobiographical experience. As I have argued in Part II, through his career to this point Pope seems involved in an engaging, even exciting, conflict with himself: in the case of the earlier poems, in the case of the later poems, the poet struggles with a dualistic habit of thought, an affliction of either/or—a crisis of maturation familiar to, it is tempting to say, everyone who has read about it; a crisis such as Erik Erikson describes in central pages of *Young Man Luther.*[6] Somewhat, Pope overcomes the dilemma on a public plane, from a distance, in *An Essay on Criticism* and *The Rape of the Lock:* the Good Critic and Clarissa join hands and, if rather stiffly, walk toward an enabling balance.

But with *Eloisa to Abelard,* such stability seems no longer accessible. Queen Anne is dead, Pope's coterie has been dispersed, the possibilities of cultural coalition—Whigs, for example, encouraging a Homer from the other camp—have been dashed. The deferential youth of the early poems has not secured the general success he bargained for. To cease to be a sinner, Eloisa thinks she must become perfect, inhuman, like the "blameless Vestal" of the fantasies that torture her:

> How happy is the blameless Vestal's lot!
> The world forgetting, by the world forgot.
> Eternal sun-shine of the spotless mind!
> Each pray'r accepted, and each wish resign'd;
> Labour and rest, that equal periods keep;
> 'Obedient slumbers that can wake and weep';
> Desires compos'd, affections ever ev'n,
> Tears that delight, and sighs that waft to heav'n.
> Grace shines around her with serenest beams,

---

[6] Chapter 4, "Allness or Nothingness," *Young Man Luther: A Study in Psychoanalysis and History,* esp. pp. 99-104 (Norton Library ed.; New York, 1962).

> And whispering Angels prompt her golden dreams.
> For her th'unfading rose of *Eden* blooms,
> And wings of Seraphs shed divine perfumes;
> For her the Spouse prepares the bridal ring,
> For her white virgins *Hymenæals* sing;
> To sounds of heav'nly harps, she dies away,
> And melts in visions of eternal day.   (ll. 207–22)

The "blameless Vestal" conjured up by Eloisa's wretched innocence is of the same order of unworldly perfection as the older
men portrayed by young Pope throughout the *Pastorals, Windsor-
Forest, An Essay on Criticism,* and other early poems, the saintly
sage whom the diffident, consummately virtuous youth of Pope's
early poetic self-portraits is studying to please—and to become.
"Such was the Life great *Scipio* once admir'd,/ Thus *Atticus,* and
Trumbul thus retir'd": the motif of the happy, blessed man *(beatus
ille),* as Maren-Sofie Røstvig has abundantly demonstrated, is
everywhere in seventeenth- and early eighteenth-century literature.[7] But Pope brings him into constant play not only because
of custom but because the custom answered Pope's needs and
desires, directed his expectations. Expecting and, sometimes
deviously, working for general approbation, Pope tended, as
Johnson saw, to regard his disappointments as the effects of perse-
cution. It is not only God's ways that he seeks to "vindicate,"
to defend despite censure, in the frantic, imperious *Essay on Man,*
after the negativity of the initial *Dunciad.* "He who is not with me
is against me."

Clearly, understandably, as the curves of Pope's poetic development repeatedly emphasize, Pope wanted to lose himself in his
work or to become someone else: someone alive in a less trouble-
some time, when the best of men were shepherds, when holy
hermits with polymathic accomplishments—Renaissance men in

[7] *The Happy Man: Studies in the Metamorphoses of a Classical Ideal* (2d ed., 2 vols.;
Oslo, 1962, 1971).

retirement—inhabited Windsor Forest, when aristocratic heroes shook the earth; when a dedicated poet could associate with gods and kings, and dream prophetic dreams of Nature herself in converse with men; or when, bardlike, an indignant seer could invoke the Logos to uncreate the whole fallen world—the possibilities are sometimes attractive. Pope clearly hungered for high if not haughty song to outsing the compromising murmurs of his contemporaries, and to rise above what Johnson would call "the common intercourse of life." Yet when Pope had managed, after some time, to accept the fact that he had compromised himself in the *Odyssey* debacle, for a while in the mid-1730s he managed also to escape the moral dualism of otherworldly perfection and worldly depravity that almost everywhere informs his earlier works.

In the satires and epistles of the mid-1730s Pope found his proper, characteristic level of life and art, of energetic and imaginative sanity based less on public approval, although he still sought it, than on self-confidence—and although, like the human being he was, he oscillated across his happy level, touching it in passing. "Happy the Man whom this bright Court approves," he had written in *Windsor-Forest;* happier the man "to himself a Friend" (ll. 235, 251), as Pope generally had become, although he manifestly had not become, nor had maintained the reputation of being, the selfless Penseroso depicted in that merely two-sided comparison typical of his early work. Remarkably attuned as Johnson was to psychogenetic interpretation, it is a shortcoming of his *Life of Pope* that he could see no such progression in the poet's canon. Johnson's remarks on the *Imitations* are particularly disappointing: Horace comes completely between him and Pope, although Johnson himself had creatively imitated Juvenal. Johnson cannot understand how the English poet, whose life was a long labor of false and true acculturation—"As if his whole vocation/ Were endless imitation"—here in the shade of Horace can find a means and a rationale for bringing poetry closer than it had ever come before to himself as he was and to readers like his contemporaries. Pope learned to write "imitations" for which Horace had produced no precedents—*An Epistle to Dr. Arbuthnot*, for example—and to represent everyday human experience plainly, particularly, and invitingly.

Which Johnson could not. Johnson, despite his Augustan, rich appreciation of the value of secular achievements like Pope's translation of Homer, harbored an Augustinian conscience in the depth of his being.[8] Although a profound admirer of what Pope had done to perfect English poetry in the style established by Dryden, at the bottom of his heart Johnson felt only a disjunction between imaginative discourse and essential values. This disjunction did not control Pope, however; and did it not simply because Pope's outlook was more superficial? With steps alternately light and bold, Pope trod where his predecessors had not, brought his muse to supper with him at home and sent her off refreshed, speaking fairly plain English about, at least as a point of departure, fairly ordinary things. When she sang, she began with friendship and the dinner table. "He who does not mind his belly will hardly mind anything else," says Johnson famously in Boswell. Johnson had a chord to respond to the *Imitations*, but had he enquired into them he would certainly have found them too reductive. More than Pope, he would have stressed man's inability to live by bread alone. Pope's insight, though,

[8] Donald Greene has recently and interestingly been arguing for an "Augustinian" view of Johnson and the English eighteenth century, in, among several places, *The Age of Exuberance: Backgrounds to Eighteenth-Century English Literature* (New York, 1970) and *Samuel Johnson* (New York, 1970). I use the term here in a sense stricter than Greene does, since I mean to invite direct comparison with the severe Augustine himself rather than with those authors who, in Johnson's time and before, may be said to have written in Augustine's spirit.

makes us feel the value of bread without requiring us to ignore the rest—or better, in the *Imitations* Pope gives due immediacy to the immediate facts and consolations of life as it is customarily lived and reaches for the transcendent only as mediated through those accessible things. The attitude Pope achieved is not only genial in itself; it is a better common denominator for a pluralistic audience like Pope's than any afforded by Johnson's philosophy or demanded by Johnson's sometimes inhuman religion.

Shrewd psychologist, subtle moralist that Johnson was, he put practically insuperable barriers between language and the heart— quite typically in the remarks discrediting epistolary candor that have prominence in the *Life of Pope* and that lend authority to the tradition of interpretation which would confine us to acquaintanceship with personae. It would be unfair, at this point, to set Johnson's remarks against the example he would soon give to the contrary, in the explosion of contradictory, very expressive letters with which he responded to the events that severed him from Mrs. Thrale. But it is appropriate to bring up that odd passage in the *Life of Pope* in which Johnson describes the poet's relationship with Martha Blount:

She is said to have neglected him with shameful unkindness in the latter time of his decay; yet, of the little which he had to leave, she had a very great part. Their acquaintance began early: the life of each was pictured on the other's mind; their conversation, therefore, was endearing, for when they met there was an immediate coalition of congenial notions. . . . Perhaps he was conscious to himself of peevishness and impatience, or, though he was offended by her inattention, might yet consider her merit as overbalancing her fault; and, if he had suffered his heart to be alienated from her, he could have found nothing that might fill her place: he could have only shrunk within himself; it was too late to transfer his confidence or fondness.
                                                                              (III.190)

Ponderously clinical, Johnson's speculations are not unsympathetic, yet he seems prevented from complementing his diagnosis with a more direct statement, from venturing to introduce a word so unscientific as *love* into his account of Pope's case. To put the matter more plainly myself, he reads Pope's feelings for Martha Blount as if he had never read the second *Moral Essay, To a Lady,* or the other poems Pope had addressed to her—significantly, combining psychology with more tender declarations—or as if the existence of those poems, written it is true by a poet heedful of decorum, does not forcefully imply an affection for her that, if at last only depending from the memory of what she had meant to him through thirty years of intimacy, could survive severe difficulties. As if when they were together, even when they were much younger, their pleasure in each other could be explained as mutual nostalgia. As if those poems were one thing and the facts entirely another, the poet a stranger to the man.

Like the work of so many innovative poets—for example, the American "confessional" poets of the 1960s—the poems of Pope's maturity move steadily away from fixed, opaque stylization toward a fresh conjunction of poetic speech with contemporaneous experience. His choice of minor genres like the epistle instead of the grander forms, the epic he thought he ought to write, or the great odes or tragedies that seventeenth-century poets could readily attempt, was an appropriate response to the crisis of poetic authority, with all other kinds of traditional authority, that the eighteenth century imposed upon him. Nurtured in poetic grandeur and elaborate periphrasis, Pope struggled with a nearly lifelong, ingrained tendency not to say anything "straight" —a forceful colloquial word like those frequent in the epistles of Pope's maturity. He almost never achieved directness of expression outside the couplet, as his letters show too plainly, and the shaved lawns of his prose essays. The line "I lisp'd in numbers" has pathetic implications; while in the elegant printed volumes of the *Correspondence,* as I have already said, the late remark to Martha Blount about Warburton, "W. is a sneaking

Parson, & I told him he flatterd," stands out as if scrawled by hand. Only after years of work and life did Pope attain relatively full candor in his verse. Yet in doing so he seems to have established conditions of accepted poetic speech not unfavorable to the simplicity, and the insights into common life, which Wordsworth so successfully cultivated. The major prototype of *The Prelude* in great English poetry is *An Epistle to Dr. Arbuthnot.*

> . . . Flatt'ry, ev'n to Kings, he held a shame,
> And thought a Lye in Verse or Prose the same:
> . . . Not in Fancy's Maze he wander'd long,
> But stooped to truth. . . .
>
> (ll. 338–41)

Fancy as the extramental muse of institutions, from Augustan epic to royal birthday ode (Pope could not write the first and, as Johnson approvingly observes, would not write the second); fancy as the dark labyrinth of the mind, to which Wordsworth brought his lantern—between them Pope teeters, steadies himself, and suggests by his example how the line may sometimes be walked.

In Pope's lifelong effort to create a means of speaking not simply as an echo of past poets, or as an ironical victim of their splendor, he was at one with his century's attempt, in its dictionaries and its encyclopedias, its fledgling journalism, literary criticism, and new, careful philology, to make its language into a forcefully definite, widely communicable medium between minds and things; to clear its head of cant and its speech of nonsense. The period's achievements in definition support posterity's capacity to make itself deliberately understood, and, in government, to attempt to reconcile pluralism with rationality. Moreover, as a poet, in his effort to turn "the tuneful art/ From sounds to things, from fancy to the heart"—although when he wrote those lines at the end of *An Essay on Man* he had only begun to do so, and mainly in other poems—Pope also carried on more than an effort of lingual refinement. By subordinating archaic mythology to realistic depiction of himself in his real circumstances, with contemporaneous explorers of common experience in all literary modes he contributed, and may still contribute, to whatever capacity we have to see ourselves and our shared world for what they are in their everyday actuality, not to mention their psychopathology, and to talk about them, to others, with some degree of adequacy.

There are several fine statements in Johnson that convey the importance of his century's, and Pope's, achievement—for example, this from the preface to Johnson's edition of Shakespeare:

If there be, what I believe there is, in every nation, a stile which never becomes obsolete, a certain mode of phraseology so consonant and congenial to the analogy and principles of its respective language as to remain settled and unaltered; this stile is probably to be sought in the common intercourse of life, among those who speak only to be understood, without ambition of elegance. The polite are always catching modish innovations, and the learned depart from established forms of speech, in hope of finding or making better; those who wish for distinction forsake the vulgar, when the vulgar is right; but there is a conversation above grossness and below refinement, where propriety resides, and where this poet seems to have gathered his comick dialogue.[9]

[9] *Johnson on Shakespeare*, ed. Arthur Sherbo, intro. Bertrand H. Bronson, Vol. VII of the Yale Edition of the *Works*, ed. John H. Middendorf (New Haven, 1968), p. 70. This passage, incidentally, a large vertebra in the backbone of Johnson's *Preface*, with its semireligious dependence on tradition (Johnson tries to base his appraisal of the plays on Shakespeare's enduring popularity) will suggest a severe shortcoming of Eliot's "Tradition and the Individual Talent," where tradition is defined in too narrowly literary a sense, too impersonally. Writers have just a momentary part in it, readers have none, and tradition turns out to be a conversation between books after the library has closed for the night.

It may be that this is an American rather than an English phenomenon. In Pope studies, there have been almost no objections raised against the dominant historicist technology of interpretation, the main exception to this statement being provided by the sometime devil's advocacy of F. W. Bateson. Fourteen years ago Bateson questioned allusion-tracing in an exchange with Aubrey Williams, *Essays*

Remembering that Johnson is speaking of Shakespeare's comedies will keep us from misunderstanding *grossness* and *refinement,* and may lead us to refreshing thoughts about *propriety,* yet I include the passage mainly because, in general, it applies as much to Pope's achievements as to Shakespeare's, especially to the level of discourse Pope achieved in the *Moral Essays* and the *Imitations* of the 1730s.

The distinction made by linguists and others, between metaphor and metonymy, seems particularly useful for description of the change that comes over Pope in these poems. The terms are used in the broadest way possible, in a way that stretches their common rhetorical meanings, *metaphor* having to do with all matters of internal resemblance between entities, with all

---

in Criticism, IX (1959), 197–201, 437–39; X (1960), 115–16. Bateson's tone was cantankerous; still, one statement seems more sober than the rest: "It is impossible to use the English language without introducing dead or half-dead metaphors, but if we concentrate in Pope's non-satiric passages on his metaphors instead of on what Donald Davie has taught us to call the purity of his Diction, we shall be exchanging bread for stones" (IX, 438). He did not explain his position very fully; at about the same time, however, he wrote an essay on "The English School in a Democracy" that suggests a basis in cultural concern. The essay ranges from hopeful generalities about the relation of true speech to true politics, down to specifics about the teaching of language and poetry through "practical criticism" promoting, for both teacher and student, a "closer *understanding* of literature, in the most literal sense of the word. At the lowest level a degree in English should be a guarantee of the ability to read English (of any period) at least as closely and accurately as the Classics man is expected to read Greek. . . . There is a natural inclination, on the part of teachers as well as students, to take such an ability for granted, which is responsible for the bad name—for irresponsibility and intellectual slovenliness—that [English] has in certain quarters." Bateson goes so far as to suggest "exercises in 'translation' (the rendering of passages from the English classics, prose as well as verse, into idiomatic modern prose)." And his point is not confined to an understanding of just the author: "Implied in the ability to

things that are similar to each other: a ball and the Earth, a king and a lion, an apple and an orange as fruits. *Metonymy*, on the other hand, refers to associations of things by external relation, by contiguity as opposed to similarity. A ball may be associated, by metonymy, with a bat or even a hotdog, or with boring or exciting Sunday afternoons, and so forth. An apple may be associated with a paring knife, or with a teacher, or with Adam, because they have been perceived together in time and space, in history, not because they resemble each other in structure. (Clearly, too, there can be in any pair of things a combination of metaphorical and metonymical relations, but it is not to my purpose now to try to single out all the strands of relativity.) Moreover, as broadly defined here, metaphor can have reference not just to second and third levels of meaning in a word or a whole literary work; it can also suggest the way in which a work

---

'translate' an author correctly is a knowledge of his meaning that can be explained to others" (*Essays in Criticism*, IX [1959], 277). Bateson thus, rather practically, relates English studies to "the common intercourse of life," as if there existed an oral tradition of literary interpretation, a confessional tradition to complement scripture and the doctors.

Bateson also, years before, had written a book—*English Poetry and the English Language* (2d ed.; New York, 1961; first published in 1934)—that sketchily but provocatively conjoins aesthetic and historical approaches, a major, almost Hegelian premise of the book being that "the language writes the literature. (The English poetical classics are what they are . . . because of their authors' special sensitivity to the potentialities of the English language in their time.)" (p. vi). The book provoked a long reply from F. R. Leavis, and with Bateson's response, and Leavis' reply to that, the controversy remains seminal for consideration of the history-criticism question. Also, besides promoting the cultural and historical relations of literary study, Bateson has recently objected to the tendency, among modern critics of Pope, "to exclude 'author psychology' altogether from literary criticism. . . . The nineteenth-century critics, for all their superficiality, have something to teach us . . . in their emphasis on Pope the man as well as Pope the poet. The two aspects ultimately coincide" (*Alexander Pope: A Critical Anthology*, ed. F. W. Bateson and N. A. Joukovsky [Hammondsworth, Middlesex, 1971], p. 294).

as a whole has been put together. An event near the end of a conventional plot, for example, will in some sense be similar to the first event and to all the events that precede and come after it: a line of similarity joins all the events in the action. One may therefore speak very generally of a "metaphorical plot." One may say that such a plot has coherence, considerable integrity of parts, but also perhaps a certain insularity as well, a tendency to double on itself rather than to become engaged with what is different, other. Roman Jakobson remarks that some writers and literary periods characteristically make metaphor predominant, some metonymy, for example the nineteenth-century realists.[10]

Of the two concepts, that of metonymy is the more difficult to speak about, in part because of the discreteness of the entities thus joined. But the basic reason for the difficulty seems to be that a metonymical relationship is an unmade metaphorical relationship, signifying a set of entities for which an internal relationship of similarity has yet to be discovered. It requires a certain openness of mind and emotional security to be receptive to relations still only circumstantial. This disposition, comparatively, was Pope's as reflected in the bulk of his later epistles and satires, which have proven so resistant to metaphorical interpretation, driving interpreters so far afield because the poems depend so on metonymical relations. Contiguous, heterogeneous things in the earlier poems quickly resolve their differences: Belinda may range together "Puffs, Powders, Patches, Bibles, Billet-doux," but from our ultimately supralunary perspective on the earthbound heroine, we and the cosmic narrator know with certainty what belongs here and what does not. In the later poems,

[10] Roman Jakobson, "Two Aspects of Language and Two Types of Aphasic Disturbances," in *Fundamentals of Language*, by Roman Jakobson and Morris Halle (The Hague, 1956), p. 78. This essay is the principal basis for my comments on metaphor and metonymy.

however, such absolute certainty and such clear-cut ironic juxta-position are rare. When the speaker of *Arbuthnot* cries, "The Dog-star rages! nay 'tis past a doubt,/ All *Bedlam*, or *Parnassus*, is let out," there is a juxtaposition of unlike items, certainly, but neither the speaker nor his readers remain quite so assured about which is the wheat and which the chaff. The pull of metonymy has be-come strong. The poet's own state of mind at this anxious moment of the poem may have more to do with the Dog-star and Bedlam than with Parnassus, or perhaps all the conjoined elements really do belong together (the speaker does go on to describe his voca-tion as a curse).

Jakobson could be writing about much of the best twentieth-century Pope criticism when he attempts to account for the pre-ponderance of attention to "metaphor over metonymy in scholar-ship. Since poetry is focused upon sign, and pragmatical prose primarily upon referent, tropes and figures were studied mainly as poetical devices. The principle of similarity underlies poetry; the metrical parallelism of lines or the phonic equivalence of rhyming words prompts the question of semantic similarity and contrast. . . . Prose, on the contrary, is forwarded essentially by contiguity. Thus, for poetry, metaphor, and for prose, metonymy is the line of least resistance and, consequently, the study of poetical tropes is directed chiefly toward metaphor. The actual bipolarity has been artificially replaced in these studies by an amputated, unipolar scheme."[11] Hence it may be that so many of Pope's commentators write as if outside time and space them-selves—in that "Natchez-Augustan manor"; write as if they were as detached as the speakers of Pope's earlier poems, and hence make little of the internal changes in his work as he moves away from his earlier poetic.

[11] Ibid., pp. 81–82.

Although there exists no comprehensive account of the stylistic changes across Pope's career, some helpful generalizations are available. According to one study, "brilliance with parallelism gives way to less geometrically witty effects" in the later poems. "Pope continued to employ balance and parallelism, but it is not the norm or dominant style of poems, except the *Essay on Man*, later than the *Rape of the Lock*. By the time of the *Dunciad Variorum* . . . Pope embodied complex satire in a more direct and prose-like syntax than is characteristic of the earlier poems; and though his antithetic parallels are still at work, they are not as closely confined in separate couplets as earlier, and are subordinated to the designs of the enclosing passages."[12] The reference to prose here recalls Jakobson's broad categories, and needs specification, but more important, I think, is the question of parallelism and its so-called geometrical effects. The question I have in mind is this: Does parallelism imply division—or addition? Is it a matter of matching, as if one were trying to find pairs, or is it a matter of dividing a single thing into two? Hairsplitting indeed, but the question may go to the heart of our experience of reading Pope's poems early and late, for the process whereby the earlier poems are developed seems more like splitting, parthenogenetic and virginal, than Pope's process later. The young poet makes his parallels, the older poet looks for them, and finds them less often. A term suggests two meanings to the younger poet, meanings similar or antithetical (that is, as a negation of underlying similarity), and he splits it into them, by division or multiplication. Like breakers, the lines fall back on themselves, take a step backward to go two steps ahead.

I can merely suggest this effect within the limits of the present essay, and almost any earlier lines will do.

[12] John A. Jones, *Pope's Couplet Art* (Athens, Ohio, 1969), p. 201.

> *Sol* thro' white Curtains shot a tim'rous Ray,
> And op'd those Eyes that must eclipse the Day;
> Now Lapdogs give themselves the rowzing Shake,
> And sleepless Lovers, just at Twelve, awake:
> Thrice rung the Bell, the Slipper knock'd the Ground,
> And the press'd Watch return'd a silver Sound.
>
> (*The Rape of the Lock*, 1.13–18)

In a sense Pope says everything twice, or more. The second line of each couplet recapitulates the line preceding it. Not only does this process occur within each couplet, with, in the first, the rival of Sol's beams answering his action; in the second, the lovers recapitulating the behavior of the lapdogs; in the third, the watch imitating the bell. But also, the second couplet reminds us that Belinda has just awakened, and the third couplet tells us again that it is time to wake up, what the second has just told us. There is tautology in Pope's celebrated concision, and the technique is nearly continuous in the early poems—often more conspicuously so than in the passage just considered—but somewhat less common later on. The poet, like Swift's spider, seems to be spinning out his parallels as he goes along, or seems to be breaking big ones into little ones. *Sol* seems to have generated *Day* and then *Eyes,* its substitutes in the next line; *Lapdogs* the *Lovers;* and so forth. Pope's wit seems predominantly projective; to paraphrase *An Essay on Criticism,* it recurrently gives him back the image of his mind. It is in *An Essay on Man* that he recommends a more bee-like approach, "Together let us beat this ample field,/ Try what the open, what the covert yield" (1.9–10), although here, splitting *field* into *open* and *covert,* he is spinning another web. His practice changes significantly only in the poems of the mid-1730s, with their "more direct and proselike syntax," their frequent reference to things related mainly by contiguity, their new openness to experience. In the epistles and satires of his maturity an alert Alexander Pope renewed his art in a manner that may exemplify the meaning of Roland Barthes's remark about literature's standing at the frontier, where the metonymical meets the metaphorical.[13]

This is true of Pope's individual lines and couplets in the mid-1730s, and of whole poems, and of the whole body of these poems, in their large as well as their small design. One may discover important metaphorical patterns but what strikes the eye is the immediate lack of such, the offhand quality of these poems, their conversational, "to the moment" style, the conversation being held chiefly with the poet's surroundings and himself. As if in a real conversation, an interlocutor sometimes speaks up, affecting the train of the main speaker's thought, but this happens relatively infrequently, and the interlocutor's part may easily be exaggerated. The conversation remains largely internal to the speaker, who no longer describes alternatives from a fixed position of his own, but embodies alternatives—sometimes ranging himself with Montaigne, for example, sometimes with Locke or St. Paul—recognizing a multiplicity in internal as well as external experience which the earlier poems skirt. Subjectivity, no longer something to be avoided, he has come to regard as a source of strength. A commentator must squint to see a progress in these poems; he cannot miss the process, the evolution of a person becoming himself, representing himself metonymically by adversion to his real surroundings, which are found to supply the plot. The domestic, hospitable setting moves through the poet's thoughts, the sequence of its contiguities hinting at consequence, authenticating his novel self-portrayal. The setting comes to comprise the speaker, who represents himself as a composite of feelings and opinions not maintained with otherworldly single-mindedness but recurrently returned to, rediscovered in his expression of them.

[13] *Eléments de sémiologie* (Paris, 1964; English tr., New York, 1968), chapter 3, sec. 3.7.

To feel the weight of Pope's achievement one must stand on grounds lying beyond those supplied by historicism. Fruitful as historicist approaches have been, and remain, they leave something essential unsaid and perhaps unperceived, as I think is evident even in so splendid an example of the genre as Maynard Mack's recent *The Garden and the City*, which combines penetrating inquiries both into the Western tradition of a blissful, contemplative garden life and into the most minute topicalities of English politics, disclosing abundant allusion to both in "the satires of the 30's. They are all," Professor Mack writes, "in one dimension, entirely realistic, and this dimension has been authenticated sufficiently by the poet's editors, and I hope extended here. Yet in another dimension . . . all play their part in an extended fiction (which is by no means all fiction) of the virtuous recluse who ventures in and out of London to remind his contemporaries of the City a little further up-river. Though the throne is empty, there remains an alternative center, and a power of a different kind: the poet-king-philosopher in his grotto, midway between the garden and the river. Under his magisterial wand, like the wrecked voyagers in *The Tempest*, lords and rich men, ministers and society-wenches, kings, courtiers, Quakers, clowns, and good Ralph Allens move through the paces of an intricate satirical ballet, which combines the features of reality and dream."[14] This sedate combination of perspectives, real and ideal, is quintessentially Augustan—more so than Pope, it may seem.

But the problem is not just that the historic Alexander Pope recedes as Prospero comes to the foreground; it is that exclusive attention to the poet's past and contemporaneous present leaves out his future, the link connecting him with much later readers. The poet's allusions are undoubtedly important, but exclusive concentration on them has a centrifugal effect, vastly enlarging

[14] *The Garden and the City: Retirement and Politics in the Later Poetry of Pope, 1731–1743* (Toronto, 1969), p. 236.

the field of our vision, an effect which needs to be qualified by the centripetal force we apply in seeking his likeness to us as well as his differences from us. The refinement of allusion-tracing does indeed bring the poet into sharper focus, except as his manner becomes less allusive; but still further, sustained effort, in the direction of concentric definition, seems necessary as we look back at him across two hundred eventful years. When modern readers approach an eighteenth-century poet, they do so not by beginning with the dawn of history and working their way chronologically up to their subject—becoming, at certain stages, Christian Greco-Romans and, at last, Pope's ideal contemporaries —but by moving backward, through the nineteenth century. They do so, at any rate, if they believe the purpose of literary study is not simply to discover what an old poet meant, important as that purpose is, and not simply to labor toward an apocalyptic synthesis when all the facts are in, but to develop our sense of what he means to us in view of what he meant.

Pope's post-absolutist search for pluralistic speech, with all the biographical ramifications of that search as it is pursued through the poems, is a center for apprehension of his canon and career that we can respond to at least as strongly as he did. It can bind us to him with a bond of articulate, unsentimental sympathy. The change across his canon, obscured by the central blindspot of allusion-tracing, is in this view the most immediately interesting entry into his work, suggesting a linkage with later poetry wherein "the imaginative apprehension gained through immediate experience is primary and certain, whereas the analytical reflection that follows is secondary and problematical."[15] Which is not to say that Pope would have given his assent to so doctrinaire an assertion, or that he ever entertained any preromantic intentions

---

[15] Robert Langbaum, *The Poetry of Experience: The Dramatic Monologue in Modern Literary Tradition* (Norton Library ed.; New York, 1963), p. 35.

of the sort posited by old-fashioned teleological literary history. But it is to say that Pope came to incorporate more personal experience in his poems than had any English poet preceding him, and that he came to do so after what seems to have been an arduous artistic and personal quest, to find conviction and convincingness in his time, the conditions of which are in many respects preconditions of our own.

Then his relapse into *The Dunciad;* but the final *Dunciad* burgeons in the mind, after, or as a result of, boggling it. Remembering *The Rape of the Lock,* the reader at first expects an epic, more or less. Yet the hero, something betwixt a Theobald and a Cibber, unlike Belinda has nothing to do. His action leads, where? The reader discovers Cibber about to burn his writings when the Goddess Dulness enters, makes Cibber poet laureate, and holds epic games in his honor until all the dunces fall asleep. Then, in a dream, Cibber visits the underworld, to hear an account of dulness past and present and a prophecy of dulness future; through the last book of the poem Cibber sleeps (inconspicuously in one line, the twentieth) while Dulness reviews her progeny and at last extinguishes all intellectual light. For an experienced, careful reader, guided by Aubrey Williams and other commentators, there is more to see—if not any encompassing action, "the analogy of an 'action'"[16]—yet soon he must confront those hard names and harder sayings. Into the notes he plunges, sinking deeper and deeper, handed from Scriblerus to Bentley to Scriblerus again, to the real commentator Warburton; to . . . the poem, back to the poem, like a wiser Orpheus or Lot not looking behind,

[16] Aubrey L. Williams, *Pope's "Dunciad": A Study of Its Meaning* (London, 1955), p. 17—the analogical action being, in Martinus Scriblerus' words, "the Removal of the Imperial seat of Dulness from the City to the polite world; as that of the AEneid is the Removal of the empire of *Troy* to *Latium.*" But as Williams says, this analogical action "ultimately breaks down" because the parody of the action of the *Aeneid* does not extend into Book IV (pp. 6, 88).

back up to the poem, now not hoping to understand all, insisting on understanding *something*—to find anything solid in all this chaos. In *The Dunciad*, what goes down must come up, to live. And in the first three books he finds virtually nothing, just metaphor on metaphor radiating from, what? A narrator imitating the dunces he is satirizing, a theme almost indistinguishable from the subject. Then, with the fourth book, the reader begins to feel a new, subtle satisfaction: in a materializing narrator-hero, a sense of conflict against Dulness, an action, an actual Muse, Satire supporting Comedy, Tragedy sustained by History, a poem surviving the holocaust it represents. Breaking the roiling surface, few but solid, these all but swallowed peaks make firm steppingstones across the amorphous.

To speak less metaphorically myself: the distinction between metaphor and metonymy becomes especially appropriate to analysis of the completed *Dunciad*. The plot, in the ordinary significance of the word—what I have called the metaphorical plot—is extremely loose, neither the hero nor his mother being as active, as prominent, or as interesting as the protagonist of heroic narrative usually is. Their inactivity takes away from the force of the action, makes the plot relatively discontinuous and unengaging, particularly between Books III and IV. And what may be called the metonymical plot becomes at least as interesting, the action based on the traditional itinerary of contiguous places visited by the Lord Mayor's procession, as Aubrey Williams has described it.[17] The Dunces travel from Guildhall to Westminster via Fleet Ditch and other stations; and the fact that the Dunces' progress shares this factual order gives order to the poem. But this order, too, ceases at the end of the third book.

While the hero of the metaphorical plot sleeps, a new metonym-

17 Ibid., pp. 32–40.

ical plot begins in Book IV. Years ago George Sherburn discovered that this new order has much in common with that of several Fielding farces, themselves loosely modeled on the conventional events of a royal levee. Very little joins the metonymical plots of Books I–III and Book IV, respectively. When a new metaphorical subplot is initiated in Book IV, based upon a competitive presentation of the Dunces' petitions, Pope pursues it in fits and starts, so that Sherburn must apologize for him: "On the whole, one must conclude, the poet is preoccupied with description of the grotesque and miscellaneous court rather than with a rehearsal of petitions: he seeks diversity of episode fully as much as he does structural unity of the whole."[18] Sherburn goes on to say that this mixture is "quite typical of English neo-classicism," but he says nothing about any special effect achieved thereby in Pope's poem.

Yet Pope has done something remarkable here, for, in a way consistent with the development of his canon, he has brought the metonymical plots into juxtaposition with the metaphorical plot, so that—as Sherburn observed—they come to compete with each other. Relations of similarity and of contiguity clash, disordering the poem and a reader's experience of it. But then, at the beginning of Book IV, the point of sharpest disjunction, something new occurs: here the narrator changes, materializes as a person resisting Dulness. The change complements what I take to be the effect of the notes, which at first beckon to a reader and then repel him, their promise of clarification proving dismally false. Moreover, the change supplements the metaphorical plot, for while a new metonymical plot commences, that of the farcical levee, there is no continuation of the metaphorical plot, at least

[18] George Sherburn, "The *Dunciad,* Book IV," *Texas Studies in Literature and Language,* XXIV (1944), 184.

none to make much of, unless the materialization of the narrator as a person is understood to signal the beginning of a new metaphorical action. In a sense it does, for the narrator replaces the sleeping Cibber as protagonist. But in another sense it does not, at all; *The Dunciad*, the epic of uncreation, embodies within it an action of creation. This action is not strictly metaphorical, as it would be if the narrator of the first three books, when compared with the narrator of the last book, were discovered to possess a similar or antithetical character. The narrator of the first three books has *no* character, as we have seen, and substance may well be taken to be more than—and more than something other than—the antithesis of nothing. The substantial new narrator of Book IV stands out like Adam among the animals, his speech lucidly significant despite the rumblings and jostlings all around him. Against the chaos of duncical language, commentary, and broken actions, the poet achieves a restoration of the original power of literalness, seeming to transcend literature in the process—almost as if a painter were to step out of his portrait and speak to you, or as if a masker were to take off his mask.

Especially, there is something exhilarating about the way the poem, distorted as it may seem by Pope's addition of the grand fourth book, may yet seem more moving to us as a result of its imperfection (like the *Pastorals* when illuminated by historical considerations)—particularly the discrepancy between the narrators of Books I–III and Book IV. The involved narrator of the last book is more than a satiric mask. The lasting power is revealed when the poet himself bursts through the voice of mockery, when the voice draws timbre from historically based denotation of its historic author's historic belief in the efficacy of poetry and history, of art and fact dancing together; and does so in conditions so resistant to his purposes that the issue of the conflict remains as precarious today as it seems to have been for him, and demands of the reader a response as assertively venturesome, solitary, and personal as Pope's.[19] There is a pretense to anonymity in even the completed poem; but unlike the first three books, unlike most of Pope's poems written before the 1730s, the fourth book is fleshed out with a poet palpably a human being even to this day, a person—not just a persona—who grows before us throughout the later stages of his career, despite aberrations and contradictions. After all, Pope had said so much out of himself in the epistles preceding the final *Dunciad* that his readers could never again take his work for anonymous—as they had *An Essay on Man* at the beginning of his deliberately self-expressive period—or identify him with a single, fixed, abstract, absolute, dead intellectual position. At the end he emerges as a poet in the fullest sense of the word, from the silence of the past a maker of historic speech that carries, a seer of partial vision with whom we may intelligently sympathize, who was not content with impersonation and who asks to be read by persons, like himself.

[19] Emrys Jones, in his 1968 Chatterton Lecture, pertinently reminded listeners of the "strangeness" of *The Dunciad*: "During the last few decades criticism has worked so devotedly to assimilate the poem and make it more generally accessible, that, inevitably perhaps, we may now have reached the point of distorting it out of its original oddity. The *Dunciad* is both a work of art and something else: it is, or was, a historical event, a part of literary and social history, an episode in the life of Pope as well as in those of his enemies" ("Pope and Dulness," *Proceedings of the British Academy, 1968*, LIV [1970], 231). Jones emphasizes the poet's excited response to the energy of dulness, his sympathy with it, but in the passage quoted and elsewhere in the lecture Jones's comments seem to complement the reading in this essay—that the poem inextricably combines life and art and thus *is* as well as *was* an event, that the poem remains as proximate and "opaque" (see Jones, p. 232) as a major event becomes while one is in the process of experiencing and trying to confront it. Poised between the cohesiveness of assimilable, traditional metaphors and strange new contiguities, between optimism and pessimism, tragedy and comedy, the poem—finally, notes and all, so thoroughly complicated—lives on like a dilemma, refusing to lie still, leaving the mind restless.

Postscript

The writing of this book was eased by generous criticism and encouragement. My most personal debts call for private acknowledgment, and some help has, I am sorry to say, become anonymous with the passage of time, but I wish to cite and thank these friends who have commented on all or part of my work at various stages of its growth: James L. Clifford, John H. Middendorf (and other members of the Columbia University Seminar on Eighteenth-Century European Culture), Herman Ausubel, Hubert F. Babinski, William F. Bernhardt, Judy Brown, Joseph Cady, Jess Cloud, Alice G. Fredman, James Hafley, Carolyn G. Heilbrun, Joseph M. Kissane, Brian Keener, Daniel Keener, William McBrien, Carol McGuirk, Patrick O'Connell, Ellen Pollak, John J. Richetti, Myra Riskin, and Florian Stuber.

Index

Addison, Joseph, 84, 119, 120, 129, 143; *The Spectator*, 119, 132
Allen, Ralph, 147, 149
Allusion, 7–8, 12, 183–84
Anne, queen of England, 30, 33, 35, 38, 119, 136, 168
Arbuthnot, John, 84–86, 143, 148
Aristippus, 139–40
Arnold, Matthew, 6
Asiento, 36, 154, 156
Atterbury, Francis, bishop of Rochester, 121, 135, 147*n*

Barthes, Roland, 182
Bathurst, Allen, earl of, 72, 77, 79–80, 137
Bayle, Pierre, 51–52
Bentley, Richard, 100, 103–5, 185
Bible, the, 27–29, 50–52, 130
Blount, Martha, 70, 72, 76, 81, 120–21, 147, 149, 152, 172–73
Bolingbroke, Henry St. John, Viscount, 60–61, 63, 65, 113–15, 134, 137–42, 145–49, 152–53, 156

Broome, William, 119, 122, 124, 126, 136
Brower, Reuben A., 1, 11*n*, 32*n*
Burlington, Richard Boyle, 3d earl of, 72, 80, 137, 149

Caryll, John, 118, 119, 123, 142, 147
Caudwell, Christopher, 6, 162
Chaucer, Geoffrey, 131; *The Knight's Tale*, 40, 46, 48
Chesterfield, Philip Stanhope, 4th earl of, 101, 149
Cibber, Colley, 106, 185, 188
Cobham, Richard Temple, Viscount, 70, 76, 149, 150, 151
Concordia discors, 30, 34, 38, 140
Cornbury, Henry Hyde, Viscount, 150
Cromwell, Henry, 118
Curll, Edmund, 147, 149

Dante Alighieri, 16
Defoe, Daniel, 129, 166
Dennis, John, 120
Donne, John, 47, 144

Dryden, John, 23, 34, 62, 85, 94, 100, 128, 129n, 130–32, 166–67, 171

Edwards, Thomas R., Jr., 1, 3, 32n
Eliot, T. S., 6, 15–16, 175n
Empson, William, 163–67
Erikson, Erik, 14, 168
Essay, the, 132–33, 141

Fenton, Elijah, 122, 136
Frederick, prince of Wales, 150–53
Freud, Sigmund, 73

Gay, John, 22, 126, 131
Glorious Revolution, 130–32
Granville, George, baron Lansdowne, 31, 33, 38, 81, 112
Great Chain of Being, 35, 115

Halifax, George Savile, 1st marquess of, 146–48
Happy man, the, 31–33, 169
Historicism (defined), 5–6, 12, 17
Homer, 99, 128; *Iliad*, 39–40, 46; *Odyssey*, 40
Hooker, Edward Niles, 163–166–67
Horace, 68, 83, 86–91, 135, 136, 143, 154, 171
Hume, David, 54

"Impersonalist" criticism, 15–17

Jakobson, Roman, 178–80

James II, king of England, 117, 130, 132, 146
Jenkins' Ear, War of, 154–55
Johnson, Samuel, 13, 55, 80, 171–72, 175; *Life of Pope*, 1, 16–17, 49, 71, 76n, 144, 146, 157–62, 165n, 169, 170–71

Kenner, Hugh, 5
Kramnick, Isaac, 14, 129n, 153n, 155n

Langbaum, Robert, 58, 184n
Locke, John, 50, 55, 72, 128, 132, 138–40, 182
Lucretius, 44–46, 62–63
Lyttelton, George, 1st baron, 138–40, 149, 150–52, 155–56

Mack, Maynard, 1–5, 8, 12n, 13n, 61n, 68n, 74n, 122, 146n, 148n, 166n, 183
Mallet, David, 137
Man of Ross, the, 72, 79
Marchmont, Hugh Hume, 3d earl of, 149–52
Metonymy, 176–82, 186–87
Milton, John, 18; *Paradise Lost*, 40, 102, 128, 130, 158
Montagu, Lady Mary Wortley, 120
Montaigne, Michel de, 88, 132, 139–41, 146, 149, 182
Montesquieu, Charles de Secondat, baron de la Brède et de, 50

Newton, Sir Isaac, 128

Ovid, 55

Pathetic fallacy, 21
"Patriots," the, 149–52
Paul, St., 51, 117, 130, 139–41,
182
Philips, Ambrose, 26, 127
Pitt, William, 1st earl of
Chatham, 150
Poetic diction, 36
"Poetry of statement," 6
Pope, Alexander (father), 118–21,
125
Pope, Alexander, and the
character of the speaker
(persona) of the poems, 12–15
and *passim* (summarized, 162–
63, 167–76, 180–82, 188–89)
Works of:
—— *Alcander*, 112
—— Buckingham and Norman-
by, John Sheffield, 1st duke of,
edition of, 121
—— "Discourse on *Pastoral*,"
20, 25, 26
—— *Dunciad, The:* 1728 version,
112, 116, 122, 125–27, 133,
137, 162, 169; *Variorum* edition
(1729), 103, 112, 136, 180; *The
New Dunciad* (1742), 104, 106,
113, 151, 163; *The Dunciad, in
Four Books* (1743), 10, 58, 95,
96–107, 115, 151, 155, 163,
185–89
—— *Elegy to the Memory of an
Unfortunate Lady*, 50, 57, 111,
120

—— *Eloisa to Abelard*, 10, 11, 49–
58, 111–13, 120, 162, 168–69
—— *Epilogue to the Satires*, 84, 93,
101, 115, 142, 152–56, 163
—— *Epistle to Dr. Arbuthnot, An*,
84–86, 94, 143, 171, 174, 179
—— *Epistle to Mr. Jervas*, 111
—— *Essay on Criticism, An*, 10,
14, 62, 66, 75, 81, 110, 111,
113, 118–19, 127, 163–69
—— *Essay on Man, An*, 8, 10, 26,
50, 55, 58, 59–69, 71–73, 76,
78–79, 81–82, 91, 113–15, 135,
137–41, 147–48, 152, 162, 169,
180–81
——*Ethic Epistles.* See *Moral
Essays*
—— *Guardian* No. 40, 26
—— Homer, translation of, 10,
168; *Iliad*, 120–22, 124;
Odyssey,119, 120*n*, 121–25, 170
—— *Imitations of Horace*, 82–95,
135, 137–38, 140–44, 148, 149,
163, 167, 172, 176; *Ep.* I.i, 92,
115, 139; *Ep.* I.vii, 92; *Ep.* II.i
(*To Augustus*), 91–92, 149; *Ep.*
II.ii, 92; *Sat.* I.ii (*Sober Advice*),
83, 92; *Sat.* II.i, 86–89; *Sat.* II.ii,
89–91, 93; *Sat.* II.vi, 89
—— *Messiah*, 27–29, 110–11, 119,
126, 133
—— *Moral Essays*, 10, 11, 70–81,
114, 135, 138, 141–42, 163,
167, 173, 176
—— *Ode on Solitude*, 117
—— *One Thousand Seven Hundred
and Forty*, 153

Pope, Alexander *(Continued)*
—— *Pastorals,* 11, 18–28, 38, 58,
110, 118, 133, 157–58, 162, 169
—— *Peri Bathous,* 10, 112, 125–26
—— *Prologue to Mr. Addison's
Tragedy of Cato,* 55, 119
—— *Rape of the Lock, The,* 11,
39–48, 58, 81, 110–12, 119,
126, 133, 162–63, 168, 178,
180–81
—— *Roman Catholick Version of
the First Psalm, A,* 125
—— *Satires of Dr. John Donne,* 93,
144; *Sat.* IV, 154–55
—— Shakespeare, edition of,
121, 125
—— *Temple of Fame, The,* 47, 110
—— *Windsor-Forest,* 11, 30–38,
58, 81, 110–12, 119, 126, 133,
153, 156, 162, 169
Pope, Edith (mother), 148
Prior, Matthew, 131–32

Rogers, Robert W., 2, 152*n*
Røstvig, Maren-Sofie, 169
Ruffhead, Owen, 49, 155*n*
Ruling passion, the, 72–76, 79,
81–82

Scriblerus, Martinus, 98–100,
103–6, 112, 185
Settle, Elkanah, 98, 126–27
Sherburn, George, 2, 109*n*, 118,
120, 123, 187
Socrates, 68
Spacks, Patricia Meyer, 1, 51*n*, 87*n*
Spectator, The. See Addison, Joseph
Spence, Joseph, 27, 75, 131

Spenser, Edmund, 18, 26, 158
Steele, Sir Richard, 119
Swift, Jonathan, 89, 91, 97, 101,
124, 126–27, 131–32, 135, 137–
38, 140, 142, 144, 148–50, 160;
A Tale of a Tub, 42, 44, 127

Theobald, Lewis, 106, 125, 185
Theocritus, 26
Thomson, James, 131, 137
Tickell, Thomas, 120
Tillotson, Geoffrey, 1, 87*n*
Trumbull, Sir William, 110, 118,
137

Utrecht, Treaty of, 30, 34, 119

Virgil, 18, 32, 99, 112, 128, 130,
135; *Aeneid,* 37, 40, 47, 112,
141; *Eclogues,* 23, 26–27, 37;
Georgics, 37, 112
Voltaire, 132–34

Walpole, Sir Robert, 5, 136–38,
147, 149, 154, 155*n*, 157
Walsh, William, 110, 112, 113,
118
Warburton, William, 71*n*, 105,
152, 165*n*, 173, 185
Warton, Joseph, 68
Wasserman, Earl R., 1–5, 7, 30*n*,
37, 143*n*
West, Gilbert, 150
Williams, Aubrey L., 1–2, 136*n*,
175*n*, 185–86
Wordsworth, William, 174
Wycherley, William, 112, 118
Wyndham, Sir William, 150